What people are sayin

Finding Solace at Theodore F

"I can't think of a more timely book than *Finding Solace at Theodore Roosevelt Island* to remind us of the natural wonders within our nation's capital. Melanie Choukas-Bradley expertly captures the essence of our political quagmire, while reminding us of the role nature plays in helping us recover from our collective stress, as we search for a path toward reconciliation."
Dr. Robert Zarr, MD, MPH, Founder and Medical Director, Park Rx America

"In *Finding Solace at Theodore Roosevelt Island*, Melanie Choukas-Bradley proves herself once again to be nature's most eloquent observer and chronicler. She writes, 'Every walk is a good story,' and proves it with this poignant and beautiful recollection of navigating a turbulent year using the natural wonders of Roosevelt Island as a source of inspiration. Readers can dip into her book for seasonal touchstones or dive into full immersion in the fascinating and restorative powers of an urban oasis where flora and fauna always outshine traffic, politics and noise. After just a few pages, you will feel compelled to seek out nature nearby to recharge your own connection to the infinite beauty of the natural world around us. With this, her sixth nature book, Choukas-Bradley has more than earned her place among the storied members of Audubon Naturalist Society who, throughout history, have been our nation's environmental leaders, writers and champions including President Theodore Roosevelt, Louis Halle (*Spring in Washington*), Rachel Carson (*Silent Spring)* and William Weaver (*Beautiful Swimmers*)."
Lisa Alexander, Executive Director, Audubon Naturalist Society

"Melanie Choukas-Bradley is at the height of her powers and goes beyond classic nature writing with her latest and best book, *Finding Solace at Theodore Roosevelt Island*—a moving, big-hearted journal that is a must for those seeking survival in our turbulent times of climate change and political upheaval. To read *Finding Solace* is to open your heart as you explore the natural world in the nation's capital with a spirited, loving, empathetic, and expert guide.

As we journey with her, ospreys, ancient oaks and black walnuts, sparkling dragonflies, wondrous wildflowers, even nestling backyard blue jays, join our lives. Their beauty and resilience are part of the solace we need. But Choukas-Bradley is mature and confident enough to confront the dark spaces of our world...contrasted with the sensitive, poetic side of Theodore Roosevelt, the naturalist and writer, whose best values—environmentalism, trust-busting, engagement and an emphasis on 'character'—are sadly lacking in contemporary Washington. These values, like those of Rachel Carson, drew inspiration from nature, not to retreat but to engage with the world.

Keep *Finding Solace* and Melanie Choukas-Bradley close at hand as you explore the beauties and the turbulence of Washington and our world. We need them now more than ever."

Robert K. Musil, President & CEO, the Rachel Carson Council, Author, *Washington in Spring: A Nature Journal for a Changing Capital*

"Theodore Roosevelt Island is a very special place, and it takes a sensitive and innovative person to tell its story, especially from the point of view of a naturalist—an approach Theodore Roosevelt would have really appreciated. If you can go to the site, this book will add immensely to the experience; if you cannot get there this book is the next best thing."

Tweed Roosevelt, University Professor, Long Island University; Chairman, Theodore Roosevelt Institute at LIU

"Over the course of a year, Melanie Choukas-Bradley mingles personal and political observations with accounts of her adventures on Theodore Roosevelt Island. The result is a fitting tribute to Roosevelt,

whose passion for the natural world enriched his personal life and informed his politics. Choukas-Bradley believes that every walk in the woods 'is a good story.' She has given us a whole bookful of them."
Kristie Miller, Author of *Ruth Hanna McCormick: A Life in Politics*

"If nature is a balm for the troubled heart, this book is a balm for a nature lover in troubled times. With keen eyes and an open heart, Melanie Choukas-Bradley peels back layers of history, geography and ecology on an island wilderness less than two miles from the White House. As she searches for signs of hope and resilience despite the slow creep of climate change and the swift political disaster unfolding nearby, you will be with her every step of the way."
Sadie Dingfelder, *The Washington Post*

"If anyone loves Rock Creek Park more than Theodore Roosevelt did, it must be Melanie Choukas-Bradley. At a time when the world inside the DC beltway is regarded as the seventh circle of the *Inferno*, Melanie has taught us all that one of the nation's great natural retreats is no more than a few minutes from the White House and the Capitol. She not only loves Theodore Roosevelt Island in the Potomac, but she has taught thousands of others to find solace there. Melanie has emerged as one of America's premier guides to taking a deep breath, looking about with open eyes, and listening to the sanity of the breeze in the trees. For Roosevelt Rock Creek Park was a bit of the wild he could visit between his long journeys to the Dakota badlands. For all of us now the park is a national sanctuary. Nobody sings that lovesong more than Melanie Choukas-Bradley."
Clay Jenkinson, Author of *A Free and Hardy Life: Theodore Roosevelt's Sojourn in the American West*

"Melanie Choukas-Bradley provides the reader with a gentle and insightful nature walk through the seasons, capturing a series of moments in life, from July 2016 to July 2017. The timing is relevant to the story, because it captures the pain and inner turmoil many of us felt during those troubled months of ever-deepening gloom brought on by the American political system. Solace was sought through escape from ugly politics into the serenity of verdant nature in some of the more enchanting green spaces of the Nation's Capital—Rock Creek Park, the C&O Canal, and, of course, Roosevelt Island. In telling this story, the author shows us the way to peace and spiritual comfort in turbulent times. And she reminds us of better times, when Theodore Roosevelt led our nation and relished special natural places a mere horseback ride from the White House."

Bruce M. Beehler, Author of *Natural Encounters: Biking, Hiking, and Birding Through the Seasons* and *Birds of Maryland, Delaware & the District of Columbia*

"Nature does not stop to mourn the damage that we cause to ecosystem integrity or our political fallacies; it keeps striving with each new miracle seen through Melanie's journey to seek solace. Her observations of the natural wonders that take place on Theodore Roosevelt Island put the reader into the hands of wildflowers and water birds and remind us that each day is still a miracle. We only have to open our hearts and take notice."

Susan Leopold, PhD, Ethnobotanist, Director of United Plant Savers, Author of *Isabella's Peppermint Flowers*, and member of the Patawomeck tribe of Virginia

"Melanie's writings are deeply centered on the joys of being fully present in our wondrous natural world. The relentless and distressing news cycle can feel like an all-out assault on our sense of well-being. Melanie offers us a way to find connection, peace and renewed resolve to fight for what is at stake. Her keen observations invite us to more fully embrace the healing and life-giving forces of nature available to us in special places like Theodore Roosevelt Island. She expertly weaves together keen observations, revealing history, and wonderful knowledge about our living world. I find myself almost instantly transported to a more awakened, centered and enchanted place.

Melanie *is* a gifted writer and naturalist."
Doug Barker, Founding Board Member, Rock Creek Conservancy, and Chair of Green Ribbon Panel for 125th Anniversary of Rock Creek Park

"What a timeless gift, this precious book by Melanie Choukas-Bradley! Sitting in my house in the middle of snowy winter, I am beckoned by the flight of the kingfisher, I sense the rhythms of the Potomac River and I can even feel the July heat as we paddle around Theodore Roosevelt Island, a place I have never been. Choukas-Bradley has such a talent for describing the intricacies of nature and she weaves the history of the wildlife, the island, and the founding of our nation into this book that was composed during a tumultuous and critical time in the sustainability and survival of all three. Not only is this work a delightful reprieve from the world today, it is a piece of history."
Dr. Suzanne Bartlett Hackenmiller, Medical Director, Association of Nature and Forest Therapy; Author, *The Outdoor Adventurer's Guide to Forest Bathing: Using Shinrin-yoku to Hike, Bike, Paddle, and Climb Your Way to Health and Happiness*

"What do kingfishers, Teddy Roosevelt, and the current state of our Republic have in common? Quite a bit, as it turns out. The intrepid Melanie Choukas-Bradley has once again delighted us with a deeply personal account of a year spent exploring a premier naturescape hiding in plain sight amidst Washington, DC's busiest thoroughfares. In eloquently describing the natural rhythms of Theodore Roosevelt Island, Choukas-Bradley lets us see the often chaotic and nature-starved modern world through the eyes of our foremost conservation president, a view that is at once uplifting and provocative, but always fascinating."
Tony Fleming, Geologist and Author of the Geologic Map of the Washington West Quadrangle (with Avery Drake, Jr. and Lucy McCartan); Geologic Atlas of the City of Alexandria, Virginia and Vicinity; and Technical Guide to the Natural Communities and

Physical Environment of Rock Creek Park (with NatureServe and the National Park Service)

"Melanie's new book is a soulful, provocative excursion to one of Washington's underappreciated treasures. Packed with botanical insights and discoveries, *Finding Solace* is also a hymn of thanksgiving for nature in our midst."
Steve Dryden, Director, Rock Creek Songbirds Habitat Restoration Project

"There's no better guide to nature within Washington, DC than Melanie Choukas-Bradley. With the keen eye of a naturalist and the language of a poet, she introduces us to the wonders of historic Theodore Roosevelt Island, just off DC's Potomac shore. Whether it is the stately sycamore, the fetching wood duck, or an unexpected swamp rose, each discovery by Choukas-Bradley in the island's wild landscape is like an introduction to a new friend.

Traveling along Theodore Roosevelt Island's shores and swamp boardwalk, and through historic woodlands with Choukas-Bradley reminds us that time in nature has the power to restore us to sanity and joy."
Stella Tarnay, Co-Founder, Capital Nature

"This beautifully written and informative book chronicling a year of natural history exploration at Theodore Roosevelt Island is the latest in the author's lauded meditations on the wilds of Washington, DC and vicinity. Perhaps more importantly, it is a timely example for reconnecting with the natural world—so essential to guiding sound land-use policies and ensuring environmental and social justice."
Rod Simmons, Author of the Native Flora of the City of Alexandria, Virginia, co-author of Natural Communities of Plummers Island, Maryland, and other scholarly local natural history works

Praise for the book from Theodore Roosevelt Island stewards:

"Melanie Choukas-Bradley brings Theodore Roosevelt Island to life in ways I did not think possible for a book. Those familiar with the island will instantly recognize it in Melanie's narrative, but they will be astounded by all the details that only the eye of a naturalist as skilled as Melanie can catch. Those who have never visited the Island will be inspired and eager for their first of many adventures to discover its charms. *Finding Solace at Theodore Roosevelt Island* is a gift to all who appreciate Theodore Roosevelt and share his passion for our natural world."

Sam Sharp, Board Chair, Friends of Theodore Roosevelt Island

"For those of us who regularly visit Washington DC's Theodore Roosevelt Island, naturalist Melanie Choukas-Bradley's new book provides a rich narrative about the environment on an urban hideaway. She does this by sharing highlights of a year-long journal she kept during many visits to the island. The journey begins in a kayak as she follows a kingfisher around the island's shoreline. We learn about the huge Grandmother Sycamore tree lounging on the island's Virginia side as well as the assortment of other vegetation and animal life on the island.

Choukas-Bradley frames her chronicle with enough history that we understand how this small island has had a front row seat to the development of the nation's capital. In the 1600s it was a fishing camp for Analostan Indians, a century later it served as a grand retreat for well-connected Washingtonians. During the Civil War it provided a camp for troops, and eventually became a fitting memorial to our most environmentally aware president, Theodore Roosevelt. TR's love of nature is part of the narrative as is his daughter Alice, who we learn had some strong opinions about her father's imposing statue on the island's plaza.

I particularly liked the way the author shares how her many visits to the island offered a special solace from life's bustle. It is likely that every hiker, jogger, dog walker and tourist has also found their own solace on the island and reading this volume will expand that enjoyment."

John Doolittle, PhD, Secretary, Friends of Theodore Roosevelt Island

"In *Finding Solace at Theodore Roosevelt Island*, Melanie Choukas-Bradley, already an esteemed naturalist, has delved into both the history and ethos of TR. She makes wonderful connections between the island memorial and Roosevelt's past, connecting the island's cottonwoods to TR's time in the Dakota badlands. While Choukas-Bradley praises TR for being so evocative in writing about nature, she herself continues in this tradition, writing prose so full of action and detail that one can imagine the birds singing, the flowers blooming, and the frogs chirping on the island's shores, and on its hilly uplands.

No doubt Theodore Roosevelt would be delighted to know that such an avid nature-lover is leading tours and educating the public about nature at his national memorial over a century after his death."

Nicole Goldstein, Board Member, Friends of Theodore Roosevelt Island; Trustee, Theodore Roosevelt Association

Finding Solace at Theodore Roosevelt Island

Finding Solace at Theodore Roosevelt Island

Melanie Choukas-Bradley

Drawings by Tina Thieme Brown

CHANGEMAKERS
BOOKS

Winchester, UK
Washington, USA

JOHN HUNT PUBLISHING

First published by Changemakers Books, 2021
Changemakers Books is an imprint of John Hunt Publishing Ltd., No. 3 East Street,
Alresford, Hampshire SO24 9EE, UK
office@jhpbooks.com
www.johnhuntpublishing.com
www.changemakers-books.com

For distributor details and how to order please visit the 'Ordering' section on our website.

ISBN: 978 1 78904 468 3
978 1 78904 469 0 (ebook)
Library of Congress Control Number: 2019955251

Design: Stuart Davies

Printed and bound by CPI Group (UK) Ltd, Croydon, CR0 4YY

We operate a distinctive and ethical publishing philosophy in
all areas of our business, from our global network of authors to
production and worldwide distribution.

Contents

For the Kingfisher and the Kingfisher Court

Foreword

by Thomas Lovejoy

Every day hundreds of thousands of motorists whizz across the Theodore Roosevelt Bridge or the Key Bridge between Virginia and Georgetown oblivious to the natural oasis below: Theodore Roosevelt Island. In this enchanting account, Melanie Choukas-Bradley takes us to this place of natural wonder and peace, giving us a portrait of the annual rhythms which await and welcome any visitor.

Once owned by George Mason and farmed by his son, John, at the time of the Theodore Roosevelt administration the island had been largely reclaimed by nature and was possibly one of many favored destinations for the deeply nature-loving President. Accessible by car and by kayak, it seems but a hop, skip and a jump from 1600 Pennsylvania today, but for that unstoppable President it would have been accessible only after a stout walk and a swim or boat trip across the intervening Potomac.

This book is inevitably a tribute to that naturalist president who brought so much good sense to managing public lands and conservation. It is populated with some of his descendants, all of whom seem to share in Theodore Roosevelt's affinity for nature rooted in his childhood, and his basic good sense about natural resource management. It is easy to imagine him on the island, excited—about, say, the song of a wood thrush—and raising a fist and shouting "Bully."

This wonderful account lets us enjoy the nature of that island throughout a year, intertwining human history with the island's natural history of which most of the Capital City is simply unaware. This is an account of the natural rhythms, the migrant birds which come and go, the flowering and fruiting times of its plants. Yet it is also an account of the exotic species which have taken up on the island including the impact of the Emerald Ash-Borer, an exotic invading insect species from Asia. The standing dead white trunks of the Ash Trees always catch my eye as I head up the George Washington Parkway at the end of the workday.

There are multiple ways to provide a portrait of this wonderful natural Shangri-la, but happily this is an account of an actual year, mostly about the nature but also punctuated with historic changes in Washington of the particular twelve months. Indeed, this oasis has changed through time, while ever obedient to the annual rhythms of nature, and has survived as this important refuge of nature right in the heart of the Capital.

Finding Solace is much more than an annual portrait of the nature on the island. It is equally a 12-month portrait of the larger capital and national scene in which it is imbedded. As such, it actually highlights the benefits to the human psyche— in this cyber world clamoring for instant attention—of being able to repair to the embrace of nature and its rhythms. It is a portrait of the tension between the two and a tribute to how nature can nurture our humanity.

By sharing the experiences of nature on Theodore Roosevelt Island the author is essentially issuing a continuing invitation to engage in the experiences yourself. It doesn't require a lot of skill and experience to enjoy, and the abilities to do so build over time, especially when you can visit in the company of a skilled naturalist such as the author and her intrepid companions.

Finding Solace is both a tribute to the natural wonders and benefits of this island imbedded in the heart of the nation's capital, and an invitation to partake of its joys and benefits. Your RSVP is long overdue.

Dr. Thomas E. Lovejoy is University Professor of Environmental Science and Policy at George Mason University and a Senior

Fellow at the United Nations Foundation. A world-renowned conservation biologist, Dr. Lovejoy introduced the term "biological diversity" to the scientific community.

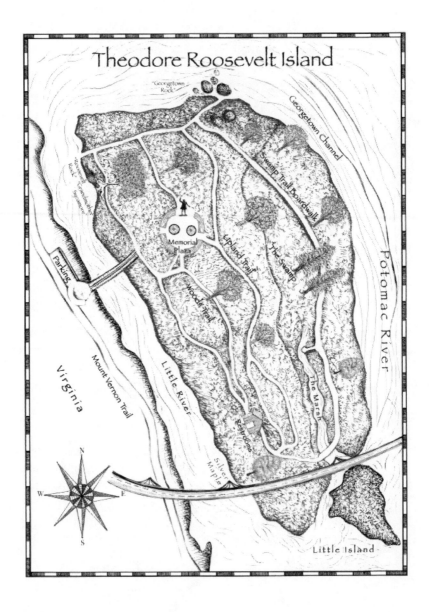

Preface

Walking alone during a twilit winter evening, I stumbled upon a question traced in the snow near the larger-than-life statue of Theodore Roosevelt on his memorial island in Washington, DC: "Whither the Republic?" I stood above frozen footprints left by children and adults, under bare black trees and the statue's raised bronze arm, as that simple question spoke from the snowy ground.

During a troubled time for our country and the world, I sought solace in the comforting bedrock of Theodore Roosevelt Island, partly to escape the soul-crushing news of the day, more saliently to find inspiration in the healing powers of nature and the legacy of our foremost conservation president. The island felt like a curative destination for the particular challenges of those times. "Whither the Republic?"—a question concerning many Americans, then and now.

I invite you to join me for a year-long exploration of an island paradise lying in the midst of the Potomac River less than a mile and a half west of the White House. We will journey on foot and by kayak, alone and in the presence of other nature lovers. We will ask ourselves the question I found scrawled in the snow as a cold winter twilight faded to dark on an island in the capital. In the midst of difficult days, we will seek solace and inspiration in what Roosevelt called "the wonder-book of nature."[1]

—Melanie Choukas-Bradley, Washington, DC

Chapter One

July 2016—Winged Invitation

July 11th: The Kingfisher

She was flying in front of me, with arcing swoops between water and sky. My kayak bobbed along the Potomac channel known as Little River with far less grace. The blocky stacks of the Rosslyn skyline loomed to my right, and an enchanted island world beckoned over my left shoulder. Ivory sycamores at the river's edge shimmered with ricocheted evening sunlight, their lowest boughs grazing the water. Earthy smells of low tide drifted up from the rocky and muddy island shore.

The belted kingfisher dove headfirst for a fish, and then retreated to the snag of a dead green ash tree near the river's edge. Had she made a catch? Hard to tell. She flew out in front of my boat again, dipping and gliding along toward Old Town Alexandria. On the next dive, the bird came up empty. She flew to another snag and broke into scolding kingfisher chatter.

How well I know the sound of that chatter from my Rock

Creek rambles, my heart leaping for joy when a kingfisher wings purposefully past or lands in a creekside tree!

Another fly-out over the water, another dive, this one more aggressive-seeming, the sound of her bill and head hitting water not unlike a human belly-flop. I paddled along behind as the kingfisher continued her search for dinner.

It occurred to me that I might be bothering the beautiful blue bird with the perky crest, as she landed in another island tree in front of me, her rusty belly band announcing her gender. But chattering kingfishers always sound oddly annoyed.

We traveled together almost to the Theodore Roosevelt Bridge, and then I reluctantly gave in to the reality of the lowering sun and waxing crescent moon. As I turned my kayak around and headed back toward the Key Bridge Boathouse on the Georgetown waterfront, I consoled myself with the thought that, at least now, the kingfisher would be able to fish in peace.

In the sky northwest of the city, billowing clouds were tinged with evening shades of pink and gold. Dipping and raising my paddle, I headed back up the Little River channel of the Potomac toward Key Bridge, feeling blessed that I had seen the kingfisher, and sad to travel away from her. Then over my right shoulder I heard that unmistakable chatter, and soon she was out ahead of me again, dipping and gliding upriver, her distance between herself and me nearly the same as when we were tandem-traveling in the other direction.

Was our synchronized turnaround pure coincidence, or was my boat stirring up fish for her? And could this be one of the very kingfishers I know so well from Rock Creek? After all, the mouth of my beloved creek was just over the horizon on the other side of the island at Foggy Bottom, and kingfishers are, by nature, travelers.

Finding wild beauty in the midst of the city has always comforted and inspired me. With our country now torn apart by political strife and violence, and climate-change concerns my near-constant preoccupation, could this island that I was exploring by kayak be a balm for my troubled soul? In Theodore Roosevelt's words, which are carved on a large stone tablet near his statue in the interior of his memorial island: "There are no words that can tell the hidden spirit of the wilderness, that can reveal its mystery, its melancholy and its charm."[2] Those words are true, even when the "wilderness" is a wild island in the midst of a world capital lying under the flight path of a metropolitan airport. Where wild beauty lives, the heart can too.

July 12th: Circumnavigation

My evening paddling trip was part of my prep for a kayaking tree-tour I'd be leading for the non-profit organization Casey Trees two days hence. Our plan was to launch at Key Bridge Boathouse, an energetic enterprise on the Georgetown waterfront staffed by enthusiastic and friendly millennials with a penchant for blasting loud Led Zeppelin over the dock. We had 14 kayaks reserved—8 singles and 6 doubles—and one woman would bring her own.

A windy forecast threatened our plans for the trip. One of the young Key Bridge staff members had explained their weather flag system to me. A green flag, which was flying at the boathouse on the Friday evening of my kingfisher rendezvous, meant clear sailing. A red flag meant no boats go out. If a red flag flew, we'd have to reschedule the trip.

It was the yellow flag that I dreaded. If the wind was from the north-northwest and stronger than 10–15 miles an hour, the yellow flag would go up. Boats could travel, but we would have to travel north, into the wind, at the outset. No circumnavigating Theodore Roosevelt Island to the southwest, which was my plan. I had scouted the DC shoreline north of the boathouse and found it sadly lacking in native plant diversity, and worse, overrun with invasive woody vines.

I had my fingers crossed mightily as I studied the wind

forecasts on my smartphone. The yellow cautionary flag seemed almost a certainty for Sunday.

However, it would be tough to cancel the trip on what was expected to be a beautiful summer morning, with lowered humidity after days of steam heat. We were all reeling from the tragic news of the week—two young African American men killed by police in St. Paul and Baton Rouge, and the massacre of several police officers in Dallas. Racial tensions in our country were intensifying, and the political gulf between left and right was widening daily. What better balm for our grieving and troubled souls than a few hours on the water, with the comforting horizon graced by the Lincoln Memorial and the dazzling City of Trees, and the river filled with colorful boats and the happy shrieks of young paddle-boarders?

Sunday morning I opened one eye and peeked out at the oaks across the street. Not a twig was stirring. Perhaps we would be okay! At 7:45, I did a quick consult with Laura Bassett, the Casey Trees education staff member coming on the trip. We gave each other a cautious green light, hoping for a green flag to match once we reached the boathouse.

We arrived at Key Bridge to meet our group of participants just after nine, and all was well. The green flag flapped jauntily in an energetic breeze. Young people in bathing suits were already out on the Potomac, calling to each other from their white paddle-boards. Kayakers wielded their orange-tipped paddles as they traveled up and down the river and out toward Theodore Roosevelt Island. Before our own launch, we gathered our group of expectant tree-loving kayakers into a circle to introduce ourselves. On the field trips I lead throughout the Washington area, it's always a pleasure to hear a bit about the lives of those who have decided to spend a precious weekend morning dedicated to the study of trees. Among us were a mother and her college-aged daughter, a couple celebrating their twenty-eighth wedding anniversary, an employee of the Environmental

Protection Agency (EPA), and a woman who volunteers to remove invasive plants through Friends of Theodore Roosevelt Island. Each person shared a bit about his or her life, and all expressed eagerness to get out on the water and experience the magic of kayaking under trees.

I showed the group a map of the Potomac River and Theodore Roosevelt Island, pointing out the Potomac's "Little River" between the island and Rosslyn on the Virginia shore, and the wider Georgetown Channel between the island and the DC waterfront.

I told the group: "Our city is strategically located on the fall line, the last navigable point along the river—a feature shared with other eastern cities." And I added, "The island we are about to kayak around lies right on the fall line, with the bedrock of the Piedmont visible along the northern shores, and the flat and sandy character of the Coastal Plain evident on the southern end. We will circumnavigate the whole island, including the outlying land known as 'Little Island' at the southern tip."

I noted: "The human body is 60 to 70 percent water, and if you live in Washington, that means the Potomac River is your life's blood. And everything we do impacts the health of the river."

The mission of Casey Trees is to "restore, enhance and protect the tree canopy of our nation's capital."

Many of our paddlers had taken part in their spring and fall tree-plantings and I pointed out that those trees enhance the health of the Potomac by soaking up the stormwater runoff that is such a threat to the health of our Chesapeake Bay Watershed. And all the other things we do—such as picking up litter, recycling, and using responsible products—affect the watershed's well-being.

I could tell by the restlessness of our group that I had talked enough. It was time to don our life jackets and the green vests that would identify our group, grab our orange-tipped paddles and go. The green flag flapped wildly and the water was not exactly smooth as glass as we all scooted off the dock and into our boats.

My plan for us was to kayak under Key Bridge, across the main body of the Potomac to Little River, and to rendezvous or "raft up" on the western shore of the island where we would begin our paddling tree-tour around the shoreline.

The crossing was fairly smooth despite a stiff breeze. I led the way to the first cove I'd identified as especially species-rich. As our boats convened there, it became clear that we were going to be seriously challenged by the force of the wind. The current was so swift that it was almost impossible to stay next to a tree near the shore long enough to identify and talk about it. The wind was loud, the traffic on the George Washington Memorial Parkway was louder, and every few minutes a plane took off from Reagan National Airport, screeching overhead.

Twenty-one frantic paddlers awkwardly tried to navigate 15 boats into a cohesive pattern so that they could see what I was pointing at and hear what I had to say. Improvisation was immediately required. I held onto a tree, we all grabbed each other's boats, a few people dug their paddles vertically into the muddy river-bottom, and everyone looked stricken and worried as I started to talk about the trees. I could tell by the stunned looks on their faces that they weren't hearing a word, just wondering how they would endure two or three hours of this uncomfortable chaos.

After some deep breaths, we started to settle into the experience. I eked out a few words about the black walnut overhead, with large pinnate or feather-compound leaves and bunches of nuts inside round green husks, clustered like small coconuts. My paddle made a handy pointer, but I had to be careful not to whack people in adjacent boats. I talked about the river birches, the smooth alder shrub, and the Norway maple (one of the few invasives I planned to point out), all growing along the immediate shoreline. Someone managed to pluck a leaf so that we could see the milky juice oozing from the tip of the leafstalk or petiole, something that distinguishes the Norway from the native sugar maple, also an island inhabitant.

On my evening kingfisher run, the setting sun had lit up the grapefruit-sized fruits of an osage-orange near the walnut, but in the morning light those fruits were nearly invisible. When I tried to point out what no one could really see, my fellow paddlers looked puzzled and disillusioned.

It was at that moment, however, that nature's magic took hold. Clinging to each other's boats, it suddenly felt as though we had become one body. I stopped talking; we pulled up our anchoring paddles and slowly began to drift downriver together. In the parlance of mental health self-help, one of the signature skills is learning to "let go." We did. Collectively. Suddenly we weren't fighting the wind and the current, or struggling to talk and to hear; we were simply drifting down Little River. As we floated past trees whose diagnostic characteristics I had no time to describe, the pleasurable feeling of the river's power took hold of all of us, the wind at our backs and the rocky, leafy shoreline sliding past. I dubbed our little fleet the "green flotilla" in honor of the color of our vests and our love of trees.

When there was something really special to share, I asked people to grab a limb, dig in a paddle, and help us to "raft up" and linger long enough to appreciate and learn about a tree. We stopped at a massive creamy-white sycamore and collectively gazed into its branches, the lowest ones dipped in the river. I showed them the hanging ball-shaped clusters of dry fruits and described the remarkable ability of the hairs attached to each individual tiny fruit to open into small parachutes to disperse the seeds on late-winter and early-spring winds. We stopped to admire the pinnately compound leaves of the green ashes along the shoreline and their winged dry golden fruits called samaras, hanging in lush clusters like extravagant necklaces. And we grieved, together, for all the dead ashes we could see along the shore, sudden victims of the destructive invasive beetle known as the emerald ash borer. Dead ash trees on which the kingfisher had perched and chattered during my evening paddle.

We also "braked" for the wildflowers that bloomed beside us: yellow nodding fringed loosestrife flowers, members of the storied primrose family; purple spikes of pickerelweed, rising above shiny heart-shaped leaves with deep parallel veins; lizard's tail with its upright narrow cluster of tiny white flowers, the shape of the flower cluster giving the plant its evocative name.

Many of the woody vines we paddled past were smothering, choking invasives, but we admired the natives, with their looser and more benign methods of draping themselves over the trees: poison ivy with small green berry-like drupes that would turn whitish later in the year (a scourge for humans but an important food plant for birds, including pileated woodpeckers whom I've seen hanging upside down on the vine and lustily dining); Virginia creeper, with five palmately arranged leaflets per leaf (a fall stunner with its red leaf color and blue-black fruit); and trumpet creeper or trumpet vine. We paddled up to a trumpet vine in glorious bloom, with its orange-red trumpet-shaped flowers. When I asked "Who pollinates those?" several cries of "Hummingbird!" rang out from the green flotilla. Yes, hummingbird seduction is what those flowers are all about, in the tubular structure and red color favored by the remarkable little birds.

As the rocky shoreline gave way to flat sandy Coastal Plain, a magnificent osprey flew overhead carrying a fish in his or her talons. Later on, the large raptor perched in a tall tree, as if posing for the benefit of the green flotilla. We admired the heart-shaped leaves and "bats and balls" fruits of the American basswood or linden (the tiny nutlike "balls" attached to a leafy bract "bat"). But that was the last tree to really captivate us up close because what we saw now, suddenly, as we turned the corner around the southern tip of "Little Island," was one of the most stunning views from a kayak. Smack dab in front of us, across the wide Potomac, stood the Lincoln Memorial, dazzling white in the morning sun, flanked by deep green rows of elegantly shaped elms. Looking to our right, we saw the dramatic Arlington Memorial Bridge with its symmetrical stone arches, and to the left the starkly rectangular Kennedy Center and the many-tiered balconies of the Watergate Hotel.

After everyone had basked in the magnificence of the view, I said: "I guess you've 'gotten wind' of the fact that it's going to be a challenging paddle upriver" (and I didn't spell out the distance, which would be over a mile).

Surprisingly, no one seemed fazed or daunted as we all hugged the shore where the wind was least intense and began the hard work of heading "home," into the wind. We were encouraged along the way by two great blue herons, who—as if intuiting our plight—began a pattern of flying in front of us and then fetchingly perching in trees just up ahead of our flotilla. Who could not be inspired by the lanky grace of those tall and slender blue-gray birds?

Gregg, who works for the EPA, stopped his kayak along the shore near a tree with creamy blossoms and asked me its identity. People were stunned to hear that it was a Japanese pagoda tree, native to China and Korea and traditionally planted on temple grounds in Japan.

"It may have grown from a seed carried down from Frederick Law Olmsted Sr.'s nineteenth-century Capitol Hill plantings to take root on the island landscaped by his son, Frederick Law Olmsted Jr., decades later," I said.

The elder Olmsted chose the Japanese pagoda tree for the Capitol because he loved the dappled shade created by its small leaflets. Some of his original trees still grow on the Capitol grounds today and they are magnificent specimens. Unfortunately, the pagoda tree is becoming invasive in our region, prompting the National Park Service (NPS) to add it to the growing list of mid-Atlantic invasive plants.

Kayaking along the leeward side of the island wasn't too difficult, but when we made it up to the main river crossing we had to paddle hard against a strengthening wind. I brought up the rear with Joan, who was paddling a friend's hand-made wooden sea kayak. My heart surged with envy when I noticed how effortlessly she was moseying along in her sleek brown boat while I was giving it my elderly all in my stout orange rental.

I must admit I was grateful to paddle—hard—under the easternmost arch of Key Bridge and up beside the welcoming dock immediately beyond it. I heaved my fatigued body out of the boat and onto the dock with an involuntary sigh.

As we climbed the steps from the dock, something caught my attention out of the corner of my eye. I poked Laura in the ribs as she was settling up the finances at the registration desk. She turned around to see what I had spotted flapping merrily in the breeze: the yellow flag.

July 13th: Why July?

Mid-July is an odd time to begin a book recording a year's seasonal cycles. July neither begins nor ends a season and has no solstice or equinox which would have been celebrated in the Old World. In Washington, it doesn't even really qualify as the "dog days," a pejorative term usually associated with August in the capital.

However, mid-July is the time the kingfisher led me down Little River and back again, inspiring me to get to know her island, so here I am. I must admit I'm not in love with July. I adore the verdancy of June, and during the month I often find myself silently breaking into Rodger and Hammerstein's classic song from *Carousel*, "June Is Bustin' Out All Over..." as I marvel over the depth of our city's tree canopy and stick my nose and whole head in any southern magnolia flower I can reach. And August is one of my favorite months, all ripe with the poignancy of summer's end. In my imagination, August is bathed in golden light.

Truth be told, I find the *thought* of July enervating. I'm not a fan of fireworks or backyard barbecues, and our Atlantic beaches are crowded this time of year. However, my love of nature always lures me out and away from the air conditioning to seek the pleasures of high summer. The Rock Creek canopy is so deep and dense that I can find coolness in the forest even on the hottest days. A perennial breeze blows through the table-mountain pines on the summit of Sugarloaf Mountain, less than an hour's drive from the city. And Norman's Farm Market on Beach Drive near Rock Creek is overflowing with the abundant local harvest: blueberries and peaches, corn, heirloom tomatoes, eggplant, fat peppers, white onions, and small new potatoes swaddled in dirt.

Best of all are the summer wildflowers. Our region is famous for its abundance of spring wildflowers, but most Washingtonians don't know the extent, diversity, and beauty of the wildflowers of hottest summer. At this time of year, our fields, forests, and wetlands are simply brimming with flowers of every shape and hue. Yesterday I began serious exploration of Theodore Roosevelt Island's flower-filled interior out of kingfisher-inspired curiosity and also with the thought of leading future nature and forest-bathing walks there.

Shinrin-yoku, which translates as "forest bathing" (or, more generally, soaking up the forest atmosphere), is a term that was coined by the director of the Japanese Forestry Agency in the 1980s. Overworked citizens of Tokyo and other Japanese cities were encouraged to travel to forested areas and immerse themselves in the beauty and wonder of nature. Although fairly new, *shinrin-yoku* is rooted in the age-old reverence for nature that is woven into Japan's Shinto, Buddhist, and folk traditions. The practice of spending quiet mindful time in nature has spread globally in recent years. Health studies around the world have shown lowered stress-hormone levels, lowered blood pressure, improved cognition and mood, and increased immunity to disease following time spent in nature.

As a naturalist who has been leading nature walks for many years, I discovered long ago that my favorite times in the field occur when everyone grows quiet, surrendering to the beauty and wonder of the moment. That's what *shinrin-yoku*—or forest bathing—is all about. On a naturalist walk, quiet and reverential moments occur periodically, and on a forest-bathing walk they are the essence of the experience.

As I crossed the footbridge over Little River from the Virginia shoreline yesterday, I felt the lure of the forested island. The trees welcomed me with cooling shade as I stepped ashore. I photographed the map at the entrance to the island and then followed the Woods Trail to the Swamp Trail, a long boardwalk through a vast and scenic tidal marsh, alive with summer bird and insect sounds, and the intermittent screech of takeoffs and landings at Reagan National Airport. If it weren't for the overhead planes, the Theodore Roosevelt Bridge looming over my shoulder, and tantalizing glimpses of the Lincoln Memorial, the Washington Monument, and the Kennedy Center, I could have been traversing a boardwalk on North Carolina's Outer Banks.

The flowers of summer greeted me in bloom and in bud as I walked slowly along the boardwalk through the open marsh. I saw more of the fringed loosestrife we had seen on our kayaking trip, with its nodding yellow flowers. The stinging nettles near the tidal inlet bore small elongated clusters of tiny white flowers. Stinging nettles may be a hiker's scourge, but nettle leaves are prized by herbalists and French chefs for their medicinal and culinary properties. Cattails poked up jauntily everywhere, with their spear-like leaves and upright velvety clusters of brown fruits. In his book *Stalking the Wild Asparagus*, Euell Gibbons called common cattails the "Supermarket of the Swamps."[3] North

American Indian tribes used cattails not only as a food staple for their edible roots and young shoots but also as a medicinal poultice, as cordage, and as basket and mat-weaving material. The fluff attached to the seeds was used to insulate moccasins and babies' cradleboards.

Green-headed coneflower, a less than poetic name for a favorite wildflower of mine, was abundantly blooming at the entrance to the swamp. (A friend in the Midwest calls the plant "golden glow," which sounds poetic.) The coneflower is in the daisy or aster family, one of the two largest plant families in the world. Daisy-family members are found on every continent but Antarctica and they have ingenious ways of spreading their seed (such as dandelion fluff and burdock "burs"). But even more amazing, and even a little *spooky*, their "flowers" are actually dozens of flowers gathered into what looks like a single bloom. So when you look at a daisy or a coneflower you are looking at multiple flowers growing in a single head, thus exponentially expanding the impact of pollinator visitation. How did the daisy family figure out, during the long haul of evolution, to gather small individual flowers into one impressive faux flower, fooling pollinators throughout time on six continents?

The green-headed coneflower is closely related to the black-eyed Susan (both are in the genus *Rudbeckia*), and its ray flowers—which look like petals—are a similar sunny yellow. The center of the "flower," however, an assemblage of tiny disk flowers, is lime green, unlike that of its dark-eyed cousin. The plant is quite tall, and its graceful lower leaves are pinnately divided and almost fern-like.

The coneflowers were surrounded by other tall daisy-family plants still in bud: New York ironweed and Joe-Pye-weed among them. I hope to see the purple ironweed and pink Pye-weed blooming on future island visits—but the buds themselves hold their own allure.

Basking in the summertime magic of the tidal marsh, I walked slowly along the sunny cattail- and willow-lined boardwalk and into the deeply forested shade of a silver maple swamp.

So while the *thought* of July might not give rise to my favorite seasonal fantasies, when I get out and about in the sunny and shaded wild, high summer dazzles me with abundant beauty.

July 14th: Rethinking July

July is working its wiles on my imagination.

Today I awoke with the early morning light on summer's hottest day yet and headed over to the lush canopy of Rock Creek Park, created in 1890 as the country's first urban national park. The wooded park running through the center of Washington is more than twice the size of Central Park, and it is far wilder. Rock Creek Park's flourishing forests have largely been left alone for well over a century. A weathercaster was issuing an excessive heat warning as I pulled into the Boundary Bridge parking lot.

Rock Creek Park and the Potomac River were Theodore Roosevelt's go-to adventure and natural history destinations during his 1901–09 presidency. "TR" led ambitious "point to point" walks and rock scrambles for colleagues, friends, and family members, at times fording the waters naked and swimming in icy Rock Creek in winter in his hobnailed boots. And throughout his time in Washington, whether on foot or horseback in local woodlands—or while strolling the White House grounds—he listened for his favorite avian songsters, among them the white-throated sparrow of the winter woods, and the wood thrush, resident of spring and summer.

Roosevelt authored over 30 books on subjects ranging from naval war history and the history of the American West to soldiering, hunting, and ranching. His first published work, when he was only 19 and a student at Harvard: *The Summer Birds of the Adirondacks*.[4] The book—really not much more than a pamphlet—earned young Roosevelt the respect of ornithologists.

Theodore Roosevelt wore many hats during his lifetime:

President, Governor, Assistant Secretary of the Navy, Historian, Conservationist, Naturalist, Adventurer, Hunter, and Cattle Rancher, among others. I would like to add: "Nature Writer," offering this passage from his 1913 *Autobiography* as evidence:

> We love all the seasons; the snows and bare woods of winter; the rush of growing things and the blossom-spray of spring; the yellow grain, the ripening fruits and tasseled corn, and the deep, leafy shades that are heralded by "the green dance of summer"; and the sharp fall winds that tear the brilliant banners with which the trees greet the dying year.[5]

Once I entered the Rock Creek forest this morning, the heat of the day gave way to welcoming shade. Wood thrushes and eastern wood-pewees sang their heart-piercing songs, and chipmunks scurried across the trail and under fallen logs.

As I breathed the earthy forest smells, listened to the melodies of birds hidden in the high crowns of trees, and bathed in the forest green, I stumbled toward a realization hiding from me in plain sight: July is the apex of the year. Winter is a resting, incubating time, spring is all about becoming, and fall represents letting go. July, the fullness of high summer, is the northern hemisphere's peak season. Here in the heat and heart of July, the leaves are engaged in photosynthetic revelry, spinning sunlight and carbon dioxide into sugar, and emitting oxygen in a process on which all life depends. Imagine if this energy were visible to us. The indefatigable leaves pursue the planet's most vital enterprise at the cellular level with such apparent grace and ease that we can't see their tireless activity, only their glowing greenness.

As I meditated on my newfound reverence for July, I stopped to admire the occasional woodland wildflower—delicate white avens of the comely and delicious rose family, each little flower showing its rose-family characteristics with five petals and numerous yellow anthers, just like its strawberry, raspberry, cherry, apple blossom, and wild rose cousins. I checked a rotting stump to see that the delicate and slender cranefly orchids were in bud.

By the time I crossed the Riley Spring footbridge on my loop trail, I couldn't imagine appreciating any season more. How fluid nature is and how fluid we are in relation to it! Being out in the woods helps us to loosen and lighten up, to let go of our anxieties and expand our vision.

And no better time than July, when the wild world seems to stop madly changing for a moment, offering us the tall climbing tree, the lazy creek, the broad flowing river, the dragonfly alit. Summer's stillpoint.

Nature may be fluid, but she is all about timing. As I heard the sweet song of the wood thrush in a tree above Rock Creek, I inhaled the pleasingly sharp scent of a spicebush twig. Looking closely I noticed small, shiny green berry-like drupes growing all along the leafy twig. By early fall they will be brightest red and nutrient-rich, and guess who will dine on them at peak ripeness, gaining fortitude for a migratory journey of more than a thousand miles? Yes, the wood thrush, DC's official bird and one of Theodore Roosevelt's favorite songsters. But for now these juicy little fruits are just being green while the wood thrush sings an aria in his summer home.

July 17th: Summer of Violence

I am writing on a flight to Providence, gazing down on the white comets of boats speeding off the sandy shores of a seemingly never-ending New Jersey beach. However, my thoughts are not as placid as the scene below me.

Will my year of record at Theodore Roosevelt Island comprise a sad commentary on the state of the world? I wrote about the wood thrush on Bastille Day, happily typing on my laptop at the dining-room table while the fragrance of roasting new potatoes and simmering tomatoes and zucchini from Norman's Farm Market wafted in from the kitchen.

When I got up to stir the pot, I flipped the television on for some evening news. What I saw shattered the peace. I instantly recognized the palm-lined boulevard by the sea that had become our world's latest scene of horrific violence. By the time my husband Jim got home from work we had both learned that a truck had barreled through a Bastille Day celebration in Nice—happy scene of a visit with our son Jesse during his college semester in France—killing 84 people, including several children. Many more were seriously injured.

Since then—just three days ago—there was a violent attempted coup in Turkey, and this morning before boarding our plane we learned that two more police officers had been shot in Baton Rouge.

With two political party conventions on the horizon, fear and uncertainty abound in many quarters.

I hope my nature journeys this year won't only feel like escapes from a world gone mad.

July 29th: Island Geography of the Mind

My paternal grandfather, Michael Choukas, was born on Samos, a verdant, mountainous Greek island just off the Turkish coast in the Aegean Sea. His love of islands carried him to Nantucket Island, near Cape Cod, where he and my grandmother, Gertrude Choukas, purchased a cottage that our family visited each summer. My grandmother was not an enthusiastic beach-goer herself, but Nantucket worked its magic on her and she had her island rituals. While the rest of the family dove into the cold cresting waves, my grandmother slowly walked along the shore, collecting shells for the large fishing net that she hung from the cottage ceiling. She harvested the mint that thrived in the spray of the backyard hose and added it to meatballs, to my delight. Together we hung the family laundry on a clothesline in the side yard overlooking the moors, inhaling the ocean smells clinging to the sheets and towels as we unclipped the clothespins. I loved that island, and through it my family's first, as-yet-unseen, island in the Aegean. Both islands lived in me, even when I was asleep back home in Vermont dreaming of Nantucket's golden beaches, sky-blue hydrangeas and rose-covered cottages, and the imagined vineyards of faraway Samos.

Theodore Roosevelt Island possesses the beckoning magic that is the particular province of islands everywhere—surrounded by water, alluringly apart. Not 30 miles out to sea like Nantucket, but an island within city bounds, perched on the fall zone in the midst of the 405-mile-long Potomac River between the mouth of Rock Creek and the Virginia shore. Not a car or even a bicycle is allowed on Theodore Roosevelt Island. The 88.5-acre island, administered by the National Park Service, lies entirely within the District of Columbia and is linked to the mainland by a footbridge from Virginia. It is more accessible than Nantucket, but it will never be the convenient backyard refuge that Rock Creek Park is for me now, or that Maryland's Sugarloaf Mountain was for the 20 years I lived in its shadow. Will I be able to love this island the way I love other familiar landscapes? I can't answer that yet. The island lies directly under the Reagan National flightpath, and planes disturb the peace every few minutes. But I have been led up and down the shoreline by an exuberant kingfisher. I have caught my breath when the Lincoln Memorial comes into view as I round Little Island in my kayak. I have walked the boardwalk along the tidal inlet and through the enchanted world of the island swamp. My heart is drawn to this place, and where my heart leads, I learned, long ago, to follow. It led me to my husband, Jim, more than 40 years ago, and we have watched our two beautiful children, Sophie and Jesse, grow into young adulthood. They are wisely pursuing their dreams and getting established in their careers and it will probably be years before we have grandchildren. Isn't my life today a bit like an island in the midst of the generational stream? It rings true that an island would call to me now.

As I muse about the magic and meaning of islands, both Republican and Democratic Party conventions have occurred without violence, and the country seems to be breathing a cautious sigh of relief. Last night Hillary Clinton accepted the Democratic Party nomination for president, the first woman in our country's history to become the presidential nominee of a major political party. Hillary's mother Dorothy, who died recently, was born on the very day Congress voted on the Nineteenth Amendment, ensuring women's right to vote, and we are four years shy of the centennial of its ratification.

Might we actually elect a woman president this year? My hopes were dashed when Hillary lost her bid for the Democratic nomination eight years ago, but Barack Obama's election was as important a milestone as the election of a woman would be. Is our presidential election history mirroring our national story of enfranchisement—inclusion of black men followed by inclusion of women? I'm daring to hope.

When Barack Obama finished his elegant speech on Wednesday night, Hillary Clinton made a surprise stage-entrance. The two formidable rivals of the 2008 campaign embraced in a hug that seemed heartfelt. America's first black president, and the woman with a shot at becoming the first female one, seem to share a genuine camaraderie forged as President and Secretary of State and fellow history-makers.

Barack's wife Michelle Obama stole the heart of the convention on opening night. She spoke of Hillary's "guts and grace," and eloquently framed a painful yet triumphant national narrative: "That is the story of this country," she said, "the story that has brought me to this stage tonight, the story of generations of people who felt the lash of bondage, the shame of servitude, the sting of segregation, but who kept on striving and hoping and doing what needed to be done so that today I wake up every morning in a house that was built by slaves. And I watch my daughters, two beautiful, intelligent, black young women, playing with their dogs on the White House lawn."

When Michelle spoke of her daughters, she held her hand over her heart. And as she gave us the image of them playing with their dogs on the White House lawn, I felt the poignancy of historic geography.

Chapter Two

August—Island Poetry

August 9th: History Lives

Like many Americans, I have thought little about the fact that slaves built the White House. I'm grateful to First Lady Michelle Obama for reminding me in such personal terms, often the most powerful means of bringing history to life. And if we know so little about the history of 1600 Pennsylvania Avenue, what do we know about far less storied landscapes within the boundaries of our nation's capital, landscapes such as an 88.5-acre island lying less than a mile and a half due west of the White House?

What do *I* know of the history of this island in the Potomac that a kingfisher so unwittingly invited me to explore?

Very little, actually, and most of it gleaned from cursory research for a short chapter in my book *City of Trees*, research begun when I was the age my youngest child is now, with the chapter only scantily updated over the years for subsequent editions of the book. I know that Theodore Roosevelt Island is dedicated to our twenty-sixth president, who greatly expanded our national parks, national monuments, and wildlife refuges, protecting 230 million acres of public land and founding the US Forest Service. Speaking in 1903 during a visit to the Grand Canyon, which he declared a national monument with a creative interpretation of the Antiquities Act in 1908 (it was later to become a national park), Roosevelt said of the canyon:

> Leave it as it is. You cannot improve on it; not a bit. The ages have been at work on it, and man can only mar it. What you can do is to keep it for your children, your children's children and for all who come after you, as one of the great sights which every American if he can travel at all should see.[6]

I first visited the Potomac island memorial to the intrepid conservationist in the 1970s, with Polly Alexander, my lifelong friend and *City of Trees* illustrator-collaborator. We found the imposing larger-than-life statue of Roosevelt at the heart of the island, built during the previous decade, a bit intimidating, and the willow-oak-lined moat surrounding it rather awkward in its newness.

Did Roosevelt ever visit what has become known as Theodore Roosevelt Island? Perhaps his great-granddaughter and my friend, Joanna Sturm, knows. I will ask her sometime this year and see if she'll go birding with me there as her great-grandfather might have done when he resided at the White House. I'm already compiling a mental list of people I know who can open doors to island knowledge: friends who are geologists, historians, native and invasive plant experts, conservationists, and ornithologists.

For now, I'll have to content myself with a rough outline of island history, a history reflected in the myriad names the island has been given over the years. Members of the Nacotchtank tribe, an Algonquian-speaking people who lived in a large village along DC's other major river, the Anacostia, and elsewhere in the region, inhabited the island periodically until the early eighteenth century. The island has gone by many names over the centuries of human habitation—Anacostian, Analostan, Barbadoes, My Lord's Island, and Mason's Island.

Owned by the family of George Mason—author of the Virginia Declaration of Rights, which served as a template for the US Bill of Rights—for more than a hundred years, it was acquired by Mason's father in 1717. George Mason's son John built a homestead on the island. Cultivated almost end to end with elaborate gardens and crops, Mason's Island was a popular destination for prominent members of Washington society around the turn of the nineteenth century. The Masons operated a ferry that ran from Georgetown to the northeastern shore of the island for most of their time as island owners. From the early 1800s on, a trail traversing the northern end of the island connected the ferry landing and a causeway to Virginia. Varying historical accounts claim that James Madison—and/or his wife Dolley—fled the city in August of 1814 before the British burned the capital during the War of 1812, using the ferry and the causeway to escape. According to the White House Historical Association, James Madison successfully used the ferry and causeway, while Dolley Madison, who attempted and failed to meet her husband at the ferry, crossed into Virginia at Chain Bridge.[7]

Was the Mason home on what is now known as Theodore Roosevelt Island built by enslaved people? More than likely. The Mason family "owned" about a hundred slaves who lived and worked at their plantation and home, Gunston Hall, and I'm learning that enslaved people resided and worked at the island.

The Mason family abandoned the island in 1833 for economic reasons. One of the subsequent owners was DC's eleventh mayor, William A. Bradley (no relation to my late father-in-law, William L. Bradley, as far as I know!).

The island was never inhabited after the Masons left, except for a short time during the Civil War, when Union troops were stationed there, including the 1st United States Colored Troops, a regiment of free blacks and escaped slaves.

In 1931 the Theodore Roosevelt Island Memorial Association (later renamed the Theodore Roosevelt Association) purchased the island, hiring the Olmsted Brothers firm to create and execute a landscape plan. According to National Park Service historians, the association transferred it to the federal government the following year as a memorial to President Theodore Roosevelt.

In the 1930s Frederick Law Olmsted Jr. designed (with his associate Henry V. Hubbard) and oversaw an ambitious landscaping and reforestation plan for the island, executed by Civilian Conservation Corps (CCC) crews. During the Great Depression, the CCC employed young men to work on environmentally oriented construction and planting projects throughout the country as a popular part of President Franklin Delano Roosevelt's New Deal. Olmsted directed CCC workers as they cleared non-native plants and planted over 20,000 trees and shrubs. The Olmsted plan also called for a Theodore Roosevelt Memorial to be located on the southern end of the island. This location had to be abandoned when the Theodore Roosevelt Bridge was proposed in the 1950s. Built in the 1960s after much local opposition, the bridge spans the southern part of the island and the inlet between Theodore Roosevelt and Little Island.

The present-day memorial, designed by architect Eric Gugler in the 1960s, was built closer to the northern end of the island. A large plaza and a willow-oak-lined moat surround a 17-foot bronze statue of Theodore Roosevelt with one arm raised as if in mid-address—executed by sculptor Paul Manship—and four 21-foot granite tablets inscribed with Roosevelt quotes about citizenship. The four tablets are titled: "Nature," "Youth," "Manhood," and "The State."

It will take some mental rigor to wrap my head around the

human history of the island, while familiarity with its natural history will come more readily.

August 10th: Nature Carries On

Today, after time away from the island pursuing other projects—leading a wildflower kayaking tour upriver at Fletcher's Cove, and a forest-bathing walk near Sugarloaf Mountain—I hopped into a kayak at Thompson Boat Center at the mouth of Rock Creek and paddled across the Georgetown Channel in preparation for another island circumnavigation.

I have three things on the key ring I carry this summer: my house key, car key, and a season's pass to every boathouse in Washington, DC. Because I have entered the realm of the senior citizen, I was charged $99 for this pass and its attendant buddy passes and privileges. The pass has already paid for itself many times over. It is so easy to slip oneself into a life vest and then into a kayak next to the dock with the help of one of the incredibly friendly young people who staff the District's boathouses. At least, thankfully, it's still easy for me both physically and because of my often flexible daytime schedule, things for which I am deeply grateful and which I will never take for granted. I wish every stressed and overworked Washingtonian could paddle around Theodore Roosevelt Island upon occasion.

Once I'd crossed the Georgetown Channel, I headed south along the Theodore Roosevelt Island eastern shoreline. The wind was blowing from that direction, making downriver paddling the most challenging, so best to do that first. Out on the river and skirting the island shore, I thought of the Nacotchtank people who resided on the island and all the many native tribes who canoed up and down this river through the ages, hunting, fishing, foraging, and trading, traveling by a method not unlike my own. Strip away the Watergate Hotel, the Kennedy Center, the Lincoln Memorial, and the airplanes zooming overhead, and the feel of paddle dipping and pulling river-water would be the same. Timeless.

I soon spotted a yellow wildflower newly blooming along the shore, an intriguing-looking member of the amazing daisy family called sneezeweed. The sneezeweed plants were about 4 feet tall with leafy wings down their stalks. An orange-brown butterfly was busily nectaring on one of the flower heads. Sneezeweed didn't get its name because of late-summer and early-fall allergies. The major culprit there is the wind-pollinated ragweed. That nectaring butterfly was a dead giveaway that sneezeweed is an insect-pollinated plant. Rather, the name refers to a form of snuff that was historically made from the leaves and flowers of the plant, snuff that was created to deliberately induce the sneezing that was believed to expel disease-agents and evil spirits from the body, thus curing the common cold.

Paddling toward Little Island past the white-barked sycamores, the cinnamon-colored river birches, the delicately-leafed black willows, and the slender and sinewy musclewoods, I came upon a log jutting into the river on which several turtles of various ages and sizes were basking. Some looked fully relaxed and drunk on sunlight, and some had their hind and fore-feet sticking out at uncomfortable-looking angles, rigidly held in place in midair. I paddled as close to their yellow-striped faces as I could get; too close and they began plopping, one by one, into the Potomac, some skittishly quick to dive, some reluctantly leaving the log, and one old geezer staying put.

I got close enough to the geezer to identify him or her as a northern red-bellied turtle. I may be botanically oriented, but I'm also a herpetologist wannabe with a deep fascination for turtles and snakes. Other basking turtles of Theodore Roosevelt Island include the eastern painted turtle and the non-native red-eared slider. The painted turtle is usually 7 inches or less in length, and the red-eared slider has a red patch on the side of its head as the name implies. The red-bellied turtle seems to be the most common of the three, although it's hard for me to tell the young red-bellied from the painted.

Above the turtles, an osprey surveyed the scene from a perch in a dying green ash. As I kayaked under the Theodore Roosevelt Bridge and toward the southern end of Little Island, the sky filled with the sights and sounds of ospreys—flying about with their keening calls, standing sentinel in the uppermost crowns of trees. One flew overhead carrying a large fish in his or her talons, in that cartoonish way ospreys do—the fish held head to tail under the osprey and rigidly still.

It is August now, with that slight break in the humidity that lets in the enticing yet melancholy siren song of approaching autumn. Traveling among the ospreys, I thought about how they would soon fly south, and how I would miss them when they go, even though they aren't old friends like the kingfisher, a year-round resident.

Rounding Little Island, I decided to explore the inlet between the two islands, and I was soon kayaking past a white and slender great egret and a great blue heron, both of them posed, Zen-like, in their everlasting quest for fish. Here was a tucked-away land of Coastal Plain enchantment, the flat facing shorelines bejeweled with purple pickerelweed, lavender-pink monkey flowers, tall purple ironweed, and the tiny flowers of blue vervain in upright spikes. Twining over the other plants was a milkweed relative called honeyvine with heart-shaped leaves and small cream-colored flowers exuding a strong honey scent. The Greek granddaughter in me noticed its uncanny resemblance to the smell of baklava.

Dipping and gliding over this inlet between islands were hundreds of graceful and slender-bodied sky-blue damselflies that were some species of bluet. Some were flying solo, some in tandem, and some were linked in the odd copulation wheel unique to damselflies and dragonflies.

So lushly vegetated were the shores lining the inlet, so bounteous were the blooms, so abundant the wildlife, that I slipped into a sweet August reverie, undaunted by the airplanes overhead. After a time, the planes themselves felt like an integral part of the landscape, streaking specters with a not unpleasant sound reverberating to the heart.

As I headed up Little River and under the Theodore Roosevelt Bridge again to circumnavigate the island, I came upon a city of mallards and Canada geese, all sleeping soundly under the cooling shade of the bridge, either standing on orange or black legs, or cozied up belly to earth. Behind them a big garish wall of graffiti, above them the traffic of automobiles and the screeching planes. Nothing disturbed their sleep as I paddled out from under the bridge and up toward the northern end of the island with a newfound appreciation for the way nature carries on whenever and wherever it can.

The tall nodding panicles of native wild oats danced in the breeze along the shoreline, reminding me that in my own chosen way, I was sowing mine.

August 25th: Endless Summer

This week we experienced another break in the heat and I had a synchronistic break in work and personal commitments. Tuesday found me paddling toward the island in an electric green kayak from Thompson Boat Center on a morning of late-August sunshine and low humidity. DC schools had opened the previous day, and as I kayaked toward the eastern shore of the island, with the siren calls of cicadas emanating from its wooded shores, I could easily have slipped into a bout of indulgent autumn melancholy. Instead, as I gazed about at the few other paddlers on the river and up at the chalky upside-down bowl of the waning sturgeon moon, I felt only the high of endless summer.

Once I reached the shores, awash in high tide, I paddled north from the flat Coastal Plain into the rockier, hillier Piedmont. I quickly came upon large bedrock outcrops jutting from the water. One large gray rock was haloed in sneezeweed. Rounding the northern end of the main island and heading south, a slight breeze from the new direction lifted the pleasant, funky, vaguely fishy smell of Little River to my nose as I came upon a garden of tall Jerusalem artichoke plants with yellow flower heads like "unpinked" blooms of sneezeweed (fellow daisy-family member), and the twining vines of groundnut or wild bean. This colorful tangled wild garden was growing near the black walnut that our wind-challenged green flotilla had desperately tried to linger beneath in July.

The groundnut flowers were mauve in color and they exhibited the charming and distinctive form unique to many members of the pea or legume family. I saw this form on display on my way to the mailbox this morning when I walked past green bean plants in bloom on Thornapple Street. Both the green beans in my neighborhood and the groundnut vines on Theodore Roosevelt Island have flowers with five small petals. The two lowest petals are narrow and fused together in what's called a "keel" for its resemblance to the keel of a boat. The pistil and stamens reside inside the protective keel. On either side of the keel is a slightly larger and wider petal called a "wing," and the two do look like small wings. Behind the other four petals is the largest upstanding flag-like fifth petal called a "banner" or "standard." As I touched the mauve flowers of the groundnut I was amazed by how stiff the petals felt. The end of the keel (containing the receptive stigma of the female pistil and the pollen-rich anthers of the male stamens) was dramatically curved backwards toward the banner, where it appeared to be receiving extra protection. The flower seemed cleverly structured to protect the precious reproductive cargo until the optimum moment for pollination.

The groundnut or wild bean goes by many other names — including potato bean, Indian potato, and hodoimo — and the names attest to its edible legumes and tubers. The tubers have three times as much protein as potatoes and are high in calcium and iron. They were a staple food for many Native American tribes. Did the Nacotchtanks and other tribes who visited or resided on what's now known as Theodore Roosevelt Island eat tubers and beans from the ancestors of these very plants? European explorers and settlers learned the nutritional value of groundnut from the Indians they encountered and, according to some accounts, the plant helped the Pilgrims survive their first winters in the New World.

As my husband Jim was flipping back and forth between Orioles and Nationals baseball games on television last night and energetically shelling peanuts—which are also in the pea or legume family and sometimes even *called* groundnuts—I told him about the wild plants I'd found on the island and their importance as staples in the diet of Native American tribes and early European settlers.

"When and why did we stop eating them?" he asked, without breaking his shelling stride.

"No idea," I replied, but his question made me think. The transition from foraging to agriculture, one of the most significant transitions for humanity—and an era that Potomac and Anacostia Indians were ushering in with their crops of corn, squash, and cultivated legumes—is now so complete that the remembrance of eating *wild* foods other than berries or nuts is barely on our radar. Amos Clifford, the founder of the Association of Nature and Forest Therapy Guides and Programs, encourages forest-bathing guides to make tea on *shinrin-yoku* walks with foraged fruits, edible flowers, leaves, and in California—where I participated in one of his walks—lichen.

On my forest-bathing walks in the Washington area, I sometimes brew tea from spicebush twigs. More often, I pour pure maple sap that is bottled in Vermont into Japanese teacups for the tea ceremony at the end of the walk. The art of tapping maple trees for their sweet sap that can be boiled down to make syrup is another piece of nutritional wisdom we learned from

Native North Americans.

The Jerusalem artichoke growing next to the groundnut vines on Theodore Roosevelt Island also bears a nutritious edible tuber which has a taste reportedly resembling artichokes. The plant has also been used as a folk remedy for diabetes. Just as the wild plants of Theodore Roosevelt Island, and the nearby shores of the Potomac, Anacostia, and Rock Creek, were harvested for food, they also comprised the region's original pharmacy. There is hardly a wild plant to be found that didn't serve as some sort of medicine, and poisonous plants were often the most medically effective when knowledgeably and judiciously employed.

As I paddled into an inlet near the groundnuts and Jerusalem artichokes, I came upon another medicinal plant growing from a stump that was partially submerged in the water. Mad-dog skullcap, a mint-family perennial with narrow clusters of lavender-pink flowers growing from its leaf axils, got the first part of its common name from its purported use as folk medicine for rabies. The second part of the name refers to the resemblance of the calyx (the green part of the flower below the colorful corolla) to a medieval skullcap.

Mad-dog skullcap has been studied for its pharmacological value and been found to be a mild sedative and anti-anxiety remedy with possible anti-cancer properties. An explosion of the foot-tall plants with their diminutive blooms was surrounded on the stump by the shiny bright green leaves of clearweed or richweed, a native plant in the nettle family that lacks the infamous stinging hairs.

As I idled in the inlet in my kayak, gazing upon the stump and its floral halo, I looked up to see a spicebush plant growing above it. Reflected sunlight danced merrily all over its trunk, branches, and leaves. As the water rippled around my boat in the breeze, and the sun rippled on the woody plant before me, the cicada chorus rose and fell in a synchronic rippling pattern.

I resumed paddling south along the shoreline, where the

reflected August sun continued to play along the roots, trunks, branches, and leaves of the trees and shrubs in symphonic fashion. I smiled when I saw a sure sign of fall insinuating itself into my summer reverie—my first red spicebush drupe. Ripe and ready to fuel wood thrush migration!

I'm sure I could have found more signs of impending autumn had I looked for them. But as I watched an osprey dive for a fish and then begin to devour it in one of the kingfisher's dead ashes, and as I paddled through droves of colorful bluets, who were joined by fleets of small flitty reddish dragonflies known as eastern amberwings, my heart was tuned exclusively to summer and its seemingly endless embrace. I basked in the glorious late-August sunshine and dry air as I paddled around the southern tip of Little Island, past the Lincoln Memorial, and back across the wide Potomac to Thompson Boat Center at the mouth of Rock Creek.

August 29th: A Poet Appears

The world turns round, awash in disasters of direct or indirect human creation: the war in Syria, and its tragic tide of refugees including many children, reports of terrorist attacks around the globe, and the unrelenting news of natural disasters increasingly linked to climate change. While the "Blue Cut" and several other fires destroyed homes in drought-stressed California this month, 30,000 people were rescued in Louisiana following more than 24 inches of rain and flash flooding.

I'm heading to the Blue Ridge this weekend with my friend Kate Maynor, to visit our mutual friend—and the photographer for *A Year in Rock Creek Park*—Susan Austin Roth. Kate and I are carefully monitoring the weather as I, the driver, no longer feel comfortable driving through strong summer storms in the mountains. As I learned on a recent trip to Pennsylvania to bring home my daughter Sophie's cat Balsam for a visit while Sophie moved into her new home in Pittsburgh, today's downpours can get scary in a hurry. While driving through a deluge between Breezewood, Pennsylvania and Cumberland, Maryland that felt like a wall of water, the emergency broadcast system sounded the alarm for flash flooding in nearby counties.

Since I was driving with a travel-averse cat and no litter box, I prayed, white-knuckled it, and kept driving. The next day, the same weather system caused severe and deadly flash flooding in Ellicott City near Baltimore. Earlier this summer, flooding in West Virginia and adjacent Virginia led to 23 deaths after 8–10 inches of rain fell within 12 hours.

However optimistic-leaning we are as individuals, our days are bracketed by an endless stream of dire news from around the world. We can send money to flood and drought victims; we can support policies and people who promote peace, social justice, and environmental integrity. But our efforts often feel too little and too late. We can choose to go on news fasts, and I often do. But our information fasting, while temporarily beneficial to our own mental health, doesn't change the world.

Or could it?

I have no answers. But I do believe in the potent healing powers of nature. When I am in the presence of natural beauty, either alone or with appreciative others, I feel fully present and at peace with the world. If we are at peace in our own hearts and minds, does that sense of serenity resonate beyond ourselves? Or will it only lead to complacency?

On the day after my recent circumnavigation of Theodore Roosevelt Island by kayak, I continued my exploration of the island's interior. I've been favoring the water routes this summer as Washington's boathouses will no longer rent kayaks when the river gets cold. I feel almost shy about my investigation of this island of which I know so little, and yet it is a place I have impulsively jumped headfirst into discovering, following the prompt of that engaging kingfisher who—come to think of it—I have not seen again!

Every walk in nature has the elements of a good story. Let me amend. Every walk *is* a good story. The tale begins when you enter the woods with an air of expectation, taking the pulse of the forest. The scene is set. Between your first step into the woods and your last step out, you encounter all manner of natural wonders and surprises. Usually there is a denouement, and you rarely anticipate the character of what it will be during your entry into the forest.

On this particular summer day, I greet the Bartram's oak between the parking lot and the footbridge to the island. This large hybrid oak, a cross between a willow oak and a northern red oak, is an old friend whom I first met here and on the Capitol grounds when working on *City of Trees*.

My desire is to linger with my oak acquaintance, but for my island story to begin, I'll have to cross the bridge. The footbridge linking the Virginia shore of the Potomac with Theodore Roosevelt Island is quite long for a footbridge—way longer than my beloved Boundary Bridge in Rock Creek Park—and it's high above Little River, with its periodic tendency for dramatic flooding. The bridge, which has no official name, is utilitarian and somewhat lacking in charm, but who knows, I may grow to love it.

Once across the bridge, I renew my acquaintance with a pair of beautiful American basswoods with their heart-shaped leaves and abundant "bats and balls" dry fruits. The basswoods are flanked by an extensive grove of lower-growing pawpaw trees. The pawpaw is an intriguing temperate-zone member of the largely tropical custard-apple family. The tree's succulent September-ripening fruits, long leaves, and dangling purple-brown spring flowers all scream tropical.

I attended a dendrologist's lecture at Casey Trees some years ago, where I learned that American Indian tribes may have extended the range of the pawpaw from Florida northward by cultivating it in orchards. It's one of our few native trees with edible fleshy fruits—the others I can think of being persimmon, black cherry, and shadbush or serviceberry. Apples, peaches, and the plums we purchase all came from across the sea.

As I traverse an unnamed trail heading toward the southern end of the island, I come upon a cardinal flower in glorious full bloom. A brilliant red cardinal flower, one of the wildflowers Theodore Roosevelt mentions in his 1913 autobiography, could be the denouement of any walk, but it's far too early in the story for a climax. I walk out on a fallen tree into a picturesque wetland filled with green-headed coneflowers in bloom and arrow arum plants. The arrow arum, in the same plant family as skunk cabbage and Jack-in-the-pulpit, bears clustered berries held within sack-like structures that lie low to the ground and remind me of goose heads.

Around the borders of the wetland, wood nettle is in full bloom, with humble yet lacy clusters of cream-colored flowers that are an acquired taste in the beauty department, yet are beautiful to me. Susan Austin Roth also loves these flowers and has taken many pictures of them. I snap a shot and send it to Susan to let her know that I'm thinking of her.

Passing beneath some black cherry trees, and some tall and full-crowned American beeches and tulip-trees, I come close to the Theodore Roosevelt Bridge overpass. The soundtrack for my walk is low-flying airplane with a backup band of cicada and automobile. Right before the bridge stands a massive silver maple tree, with shaggy gray bark and delicate, deeply sinused leaves, which are all silvery underneath and gracefully swaying in the summer breeze.

This silver maple is serving a dramatic *feng shui* function, acting as a strong protector of the island forest, holding back the malevolent energy of the bridge.

American elms and redbud trees lead me to the place my heart most yearningly seeks: the Swamp Trail boardwalk. Entering the open landscape of the tidal marsh surrounding the boardwalk entrance, an Everglade-esque world of rushes, sedges, and grasses, I'm immediately greeted by August blooms that were mere buds in my July walk story: tall Joe-Pye-weed with large round clusters of dusky pink blooms haloed in insect pollinators; purple New York ironweed, wearing the flitting tiara of a yellow and black tiger swallowtail butterfly; green-headed coneflower still blooming with its sunny yellow rays surrounding a green central disk.

As I walk slowly along the boardwalk, common whitetail dragonflies alight and fly in front of me, and I hear the beseeching cries of Little Island's ospreys, just to the south. The tall purple-speckled stalks of the deadly poisonous water hemlock, cousin of *the* poison hemlock that purportedly brought about Socrates' demise *and* the edible carrot, still bear their last late-summer umbels several feet above the swampy terrain. Cattails dance in the breeze and—to add an extra layer of historic magic to the scene—wild rice, staple of the Nacotchtank people, is visible in the distance.

As I slowly walk north along the boardwalk, I take the purple of the abundant New York ironweed straight to my heart along with the sky blue of the three-petaled Virginia dayflowers springing up from the marsh.

When I come upon a bench I sit, in order to bask in beauty. I remain for a good long while, no time-tracking. Then I see a young woman walking toward me from the north, reading a book as she traverses the boardwalk. She has mastered the art of simultaneous walking and reading, and as she comes closer I see that there are inky black images of what look like Joshua trees on her book's cover.

When she sees me she sighs and asks: "Do you know how much farther it is?" adding, "The signage here isn't very good."

I have remembered to bring a map I printed out from a National Park Service website and I show it to her and advise her to avoid certain wrong turns on the way back.

"I got lost on this island with a friend once," I say to her, "and it got dark and took us a long time to find our way back."

My botanist friend Cris Fleming and I were mortified to be lost on the island a few years ago as we both pride ourselves on having finely honed senses of direction. But we had to admit we were lost when the Washington Monument was beaming through the dark from the opposite direction from where we thought it should be! After more than an hour of stumbling down wrong trails in the dark, with a growing sense of anxiety, we finally found our way back to the footbridge and the Virginia shore.

The young woman sits down next to me and we begin to talk. I learn that her name is Disha Banik and she is a brand-new Berkeley graduate who is starting an antitrust job at the Department of Justice the following week. I volunteer information about other wild places in the area—Rock Creek Park, Great Falls and the Billy Goat trails, Sugarloaf Mountain. Truth be told, I can't stop myself from offering the information.

I ask her about the book she now holds in her lap.

It is a Pulitzer-prize winning book of poetry by Kay Ryan, a poet unfamiliar to me, although I see on the book cover that she was the poet laureate of the United States from 2008 to 2010. I learn that Disha has all sorts of plans and goals for her new life in Washington, including finding poetry readings and workshops.

She hesitates for a moment, as if second-guessing herself before speaking. Then she says, "Do you want to read this one poem in my book?"

I always prefer to hear poetry read aloud and I ask her, "Will you read it to me?"

"Sure," she says, after the slightest hesitation. "I have to warn you though, that although this is a very good poem, it doesn't have a happy ending."

Since I bought the book after leaving the island, I was able to read the evocative poem again. It's called "Easter Island," and is one of the "new" poems in the collection of "new and selected poems" titled *The Best of It*. In short haunting phrases, our former poet laureate tells the story of how the placement of the famous monolithic heads of Easter Island displaced forest trees.

Between the poem's title and verse is the following blurb:

> The people of the island built those amazing stone statues, and in the process cut down every last tree. No trees, no wood for houses and fires; no protection from erosion; no useful species, and so on.
>
> —Jon Carroll, *San Francisco Chronicle*[8]

I ask Disha to read the poem twice, and when she finishes reading the second time there are tears in her eyes. "I can't believe I'm crying with a total stranger," she says.

Trying to offer some reassurance, I tell Disha: "I have met so many people in the woods." I can picture the thought-bubble above her head wondering just how crazy I might be. I tell her how these woodland introductions have given rise to all kinds of collaborative endeavors, including books, and I can see her relaxing a little and trusting her initial instinct to share the poem.

I wish Disha well in her new life and her new job, we exchange contact information, and I invite her to get in touch with me any time with questions about the wild parts of the city. We both arise from the boardwalk bench and say our goodbyes. She heads south and I head north, each carrying our own story of the other.

This walk story has had its denouement. But it will also have what I might view in hindsight as a rather too-tidy conclusion.

I walk out from the Swamp Trail and onto a rock outcrop facing the Georgetown waterfront, rocks that I have paddled past many times this summer. The rocks are slimy in the tide zone, there are bottles and cans caught along their upriver sides, and the water is not entirely pristine. But do I focus on this or the beauty of this powerful river, reliably flowing from the Appalachian Mountains to the Chesapeake Bay? There's a question I can answer.

I have to consult my map to find the great plaza with the 17-foot bronze statue of Roosevelt, arm upstretched. It's not exactly Easter Island, but I can't ignore the message of the poem, or the rather uncomfortable feeling I've always had in the presence of the larger-than-life statue with its impervious plaza and surrounding moat. What would the man who hunted and cattle-ranched in the Dakota badlands as a young man, and explored the Amazonian River of Doubt as an older one, the president who preserved millions of acres of public lands, think of this huge statue of himself plunked in the midst of an otherwise wild island memorial? I wonder.

Roosevelt was a deeply thoughtful and evocative writer on wide-ranging topics and ideas, and I gravitate to one of the four tall tablets behind the statue bearing his words engraved in granite. I read:

NATURE

There is delight in the hardy life of the open

There are no words that can tell the hidden spirit of the Wilderness; that can reveal its mystery, its melancholy and its charm

The nation behaves well if it treats the Natural Resources as assets which it must turn over to the Next Generation increased and not impaired in value

All of those words slide down like honey. But at the bottom of the rock tablet is something I'll have to ponder further, while searching for its context: "Conservation means Development as much as it does Protection."[9]

I guess every story closes with some potential for a sequel.

August 31st: Paddling with Sadie

"Sadie Dingfelder will write about anything, but she especially loves art, science, wildlife and quirky people." That's her reporter's bio on the *Washington Post* website. As I hurried across Rock Creek's southernmost footbridge to meet her at Thompson Boat Center for a trip around Theodore Roosevelt Island, I figured I had at least two of the bases covered for the river adventure I'd planned for our first in-person meeting. We could certainly count on wildlife—and quirky was not in question.

Sadie has interviewed me for three of her offbeat stories in *The Washington Post Express* this past year, the most recent two being "Who Needs the Corpse Flower?" and "What Kind of Cherry Blossom Are You?" We had never met in person, but we spontaneously gave each other a big warm hug next to the dock because I think it's safe to say we had already figured out that we were kindred spirits. Two wacky women who love nature and have managed to find a toehold as writers in the staid capital of Washington. Separated by a few decades age-wise, which, at least to me, seemed instantly irrelevant.

Tucked into our single kayaks, we paddled straight across the river on a late-summer morning promising heat. I told Sadie she had good bird karma when ospreys and great blue herons appeared in all their splendor and gawky grace. She told me that she owns a blowup kayak, which she frequently launches on the Anacostia before dawn.

Sadie and I spent the morning paddling the south-first circumnavigation route, down toward the Kennedy Center and Lincoln Memorial and back up along the Virginia-facing side of the island. The tide was low and I was disappointed that we couldn't get closer to the wildflowers growing in great profusion along the shoreline. As if I'd forgotten to sweep the kitchen floor or had a stain on my living-room rug, I felt apologetic about the glaring mats of invasive feathery *Hydrilla* floating all around the island and presenting themselves to Sadie's gaze because of low tide. But every cloud has a silver lining, and the *Hydrilla* mats supported the open yellow flowers of delicate water stargrass, an emergent species of plant (a plant growing in water with plant parts above the surface). Bluets and amberwings danced above the floating yellow stars, creating a tapestry of yellow, blue, and red.

I spotted my second migrating solitary sandpiper of the week, an identification confirmed by my dad, a lifelong birder, via email and also serendipitously by Vermont naturalist Mary Holland's nature blog that arrived in my inbox the morning of Sadie's and my trip. Solitary sandpipers are, well, solitary and they are in migration mode now. I will always be a plant person, but the island is luring me more and more into the land of the birder, where Sadie resides.

As we happily paddled around the island, Sadie and I shared details of our lives. Quirky people come with juicy life-stories, big and small. Sadie is not only a young up-and-coming reporter for the *Washington Post*. She's also a violinist and a standup comic. By the time we got back to the dock we were old friends, already talking about our next wild adventure, which will have to wait until after Sadie's wedding to Steve Hay and their Hawaiian honeymoon.

Chapter Three

September—Nature Journaling

September 15th: Engagement

Recently, a friend asked me to sum up how I interact with the world in a single word. After fumbling around with a few incoherent thought-threads, I stumbled upon my perfect one-word summation: *engagement*.

I'm underwhelmed just now by my dictionary's definition of the word *engage*: "to keep busy, occupy." To me, it has a more intimate and connective meaning. In my own life, wherever I'm *engaged* is where my energy flows, as energy simultaneously circles back to me. Engagement with nature feels spiritually, emotionally, and physically nourishing and uplifting; engagement with electronics often has a more jagged edge. It occurred to me recently that when I'm completely idle in the woods I feel that I'm fully alive and right where I belong. I would never consider a moment sitting under a tree wasted time. And yet, I can spend five hours working at my computer, as industrious as can be, and when I get up and walk away, I feel as though I've wasted those hours. When I'm engaged in writing something meaningful to me like this island account, I do feel fully present and don't have a wasted-time hangover afterwards. But when I'm planning and prepping and catching up on email, the engagement often feels fractured and enervating.

I'm finding it challenging to engage with Theodore Roosevelt Island as much as I yearn to do so. It's primarily a distance thing. Rock Creek Park is five minutes away; the island takes much more time to approach. It's a 30-minute drive to Key Bridge Boathouse or Thompson Boat Center, and parking at both places can be difficult. To walk the island on foot I have to drive to northern Virginia to access the footbridge. A strained tendon has made the island impossible to access by bicycle, hopefully a temporary situation.

Last week, life threw me a career curve when some of my upcoming events were canceled with little explanation from the sponsoring non-profit, fostering feelings of rejection and *disengagement*. As I nursed my bruised feelings, my wholehearted desire was for *engagement* with the island.

Tuesday afternoon I managed to sneak onto the Rock Creek Parkway from Massachusetts Avenue at 3:44, with one minute to spare before the one-way traffic pattern kicked in. By the time I signed in at Thompson Boat Center I was informed that I had to be back in an hour and 20 minutes, not enough time for a leisurely trip around the island.

As I headed down to the dock to pick up my life jacket and kayak paddle, high-school crew teams were launching their shells. This was a surer sign of approaching autumn than the hot and humid afternoon air could muster. The tide was high, and a gibbous harvest moon was crossing the sky.

Only recently did it dawn on me that Rock Creek must be tidal near its mouth. As much as I wanted to kayak to the island and learn the answer to my burning question — "Are the ospreys still here?"—I couldn't resist the lure of high tide in lower Rock Creek.

Back at the boathouse, the gentleman at the registration desk had advised me against paddling up Rock Creek, but, when pressed, he couldn't offer a convincing argument against it.

So, without much hesitation I turned my kayak to the left beyond the dock and up the creek just past Milepost Zero of the Chesapeake and Ohio (C&O) Canal. It felt a bit illicit, but it was exciting to paddle an unfamiliar stretch of the beloved creek. Many of the trees overhanging the water were non-native invasives—ailanthus, white mulberry, mimosa, paulownia, Norway maple—lovely trees all, which I would thrill to see in their home environments. Invasive shrubs, including porcelain berry, were also lushly growing. But amid the tangle of invasives, native trees prevailed—bone-white sycamores, silver maples, and boxelders bearing gold-green elongated clusters of the paired winged seeds called samaras.

The overall vegetative effect was decidedly jungly, but traveling upstream, surreal-looking contemporary office buildings followed one upon the other over my left shoulder. As I paddled under the K Street overpass, something caught my eye in the water next to me. A water snake? Nope, it was a turtle slogging along, and he or she quickly dove down after too much verbal attention from me.

As I paddled under the Whitehurst Freeway, a green heron zoomed beneath and beyond the overpass. I had an "aha" moment when I realized that *if* the Theodore Roosevelt Island kingfishers and Rock Creek kingfishers are one and the same, flight beneath these overpasses would be part of their journey.

I got as far as Lock 1 of the C&O Canal, where I turned my kayak around and headed back down the creek and over to the island. As I left intimate tree-lined Rock Creek and began crossing the wide blue expanse of the Potomac, I scanned the sky for ospreys and came up empty. The whole expanse of sky, from north of Key Bridge to beyond Memorial Bridge, was ospreyless, and the cold gibbous moon high in the sky had nothing to say about it.

"I *missed* them; I *missed* their departure," I sadly told myself, feeling disengaged from the life of the island due to my prolonged absence. Then, as I neared the eastern shore, I heard the familiar keening call, that high-pitched almost mousy squeal that seems a bit incongruous for the regal bird. As I paddled down toward Little Island, more ospreys appeared, flying about, hovering over the river in search of fish, and standing sentinel in the crowns of dead and dying green ashes.

As I came to the Theodore Roosevelt Bridge underpass, a log lying in shallow water sported two snoozing mallards and a cormorant. The cormorant flew off as I approached. The day became a heron/egret triple header when a great blue heron flew around the tip of Little Island and then a great egret with brilliant white feathers winged its way south toward Alexandria. Wildflowers spilled from the shoreline—a colorful trio of yellow sneezeweeds, lavender mistflowers, and one brilliant red cardinal flower. I could hear my friend Liz Wedam saying, "Every room should have something red in it," as I thought, So should every island shoreline.

I knew I was going to be late getting back to the dock but I couldn't resist the temptation to paddle into the Little Island inlet, where the tiny white flowers of American water horehound bloomed. I saw abundant capsules of swamp rose mallow and wondered how in the world I missed those showy *Hibiscus* genus blooms this summer.

As evening settled in, the ambience of rush-hour traffic on the bridges, and the planes and helicopters overhead, blended surprisingly harmoniously with the young people rowing on the river and the birds winging past. As I drank in the beauty of the island with its flower-lined shores, I felt deeply and fully *engaged*. I hope it will be a long and happy engagement, following that unexpected kingfisher proposal last July.

September 19th: Nature Journaling

As we crossed the footbridge on a warm late-summer morning of sun and clouds, a day just shy of the autumn equinox, my friend Kate Maynor gave me an assignment: "Find a plant you don't know." Once I'd found it, we'd settle ourselves into our portable forest-bathing stools and she would teach me the art of nature journaling.

As we walked, I was on a dual mission: to find the plant, and to share my newfound love of the island with my friend. Just as I had gone to California earlier this year to learn about forest bathing in Sonoma County, Kate had gone to California to learn nature journaling from a master in the Sierras. I was already pumped after my visit to the art store to purchase the journal and pencils Kate had recommended while we were sitting in Susan Austin Roth's garden in the Blue Ridge Mountains together earlier this month. While hummingbirds and goldfinches flitted about Susan's feeders, and butterflies hovered over her flowers, I took meticulous notes about Kate's recommendations for art supplies.

Kate is an art conservator at the Smithsonian's Museum of American Art and she's just getting launched as a nature journaling instructor. I was her lucky guinea pig.

After crossing the bridge, Kate and I stopped to admire the tall American basswoods that serve as island greeters. Turning to the right we followed a path I'm learning to love. It moseys down toward Little Island, hooking up with the Swamp Trail near the Theodore Roosevelt Bridge. I wanted to find that mystery plant, but I also wanted Kate to witness the magic of the tall forest trees we walked beneath and the adjacent wetlands, alive with bird and insect songs, stretching tantalizingly out toward Little River.

She didn't let me down. She loved the scene and she noticed

three woody plants I had failed to see in my rather hasty trips down this particular trail: bitternut hickory, hackberry, and bladdernut. Her observations delighted me, but I was failing to delight her in my search for the mystery plant. I walked out into the wetland on a fallen tree and I might have found something there, but because Kate didn't follow me, I quickly intuited that this was not the sort of setting she had in mind for journaling.

We continued on toward the Theodore Roosevelt Bridge and then turned left (north) onto the boardwalk into the tidal marsh and the swamp. I was quietly thrilled, as always, by the marsh, in hearing distance of the Little Island ospreys, who were still in residence with their keening calls. A great blue heron rose and flew, leaving behind a bright red cardinal flower and some purple ironweed. Here was spread out all the natural magic one could want for nature journaling, right? But not necessarily. Kate said we would want to sit in the shade. Feeling a bit crestfallen, I worried that I was letting her down twofold: no shade and no mystery plant.

But just as I was giving up hope, my heart leapt at the sight of a small, three-petaled pink flower that I had never seen before. It was a delicate little flower on a grass-like stalk, and although this wasn't part of the assignment, I couldn't help whipping out my field guide to try to identify it. But it was not in the field guide I carried, which made me 1) hope that this meant it was a southern Coastal Plain plant that I had just never come upon, being largely a Piedmont person, and 2) worry that it was yet another new invasive.

Kate had never seen it either. We had found our plant. Now we required shade and there was none to be found around the pink flower. However, looking ahead we noticed the flower blooming all along the boardwalk and there were some silver maples just beyond them. If we got lucky, perhaps our flower would be growing near the shade. Bingo! It was and we set up shop, hauling our nature journals out from our packs, arraying our colored pencils around us, and setting up and settling into our tripod stools.

Kate opened the journaling session with some simple breathing and grounding exercises, which were interrupted by four exuberant children who had careened down the boardwalk from the north with their parents. They all wanted to look through my binoculars, which were sitting on a bench next to me—the very bench where I had heard the words of the poem "Easter Island" read aloud, twice, not so long ago. Nothing like a little childhood joy and memory of poetry to get you in the mood to breathe, relax, and *engage*, once the commotion moved along.

Kate shared calming words from Thich Nhat Hanh: "Breathing in, I calm my body. Breathing out, I smile. Dwelling in the present moment, I know this is a wonderful moment!"[10]

I instantly settled into the wonder of the moment, the tantalizing mix of sun and clouds, the silvery undersides of the maple leaves trembling in the breeze and creating dappled shade, the watery world below the boardwalk reflecting it all. The gentle chorus of late-summer insects was punctuated by the periodic airplanes, all of a piece. My husband might have been in one of those planes, flying off to Jacksonville for a conference on the Gulf coast.

Kate read a short quote from one of my favorite authors, Terry Tempest Williams, words that went straight to my homebody heart: "It just may be that the most radical act we can commit is to stay home."[11] She then shared a quote from her beloved journaling teacher, John ("Jack") Muir Laws: "You don't have to be on the Serengeti to find wonder."[12]

I was giddy with anticipation as I opened up my new black journal with its black wire binding, ready to absorb Kate's Sierra-inspired journaling lesson. After jotting down what Kate called the "metadata" [Theodore Roosevelt Island, September 18, 2016; The Swamp Trail Boardwalk; 82 degrees Fahrenheit (28 Celsius):

sun and clouds, very humid (73%); light cricket backdrop with airplane punctuation; gentle breeze] she shared with me the three observations Jack had taught her to make for each plant or natural subject of the nature journal: "I notice." "I wonder." And "It reminds me of." "INIWIRMO," pronounced "innywirmo."

I noticed that the mystery plant was about 12–15 inches tall, with alternate clasping leaves and jointed stem. The flowers, which I meticulously drew with my colored pencils, had three petals that were rounded at the tips and intriguing tiny reproductive parts that seemed to have two different sets of stamens and a baffling pistil. *I noticed* the plant's habitat, which was watery parts of the swamp, growing near cattails, New York ironweed, Virginia dayflowers, spicebush, silver maple, and (planted) bald-cypress. *I wondered* what the heck it was and whether it was invasive or native. And the leaves *reminded me of* grass and the flowers *reminded me of* dayflowers.

After drawing our flowers and doing some leaf rubbings, we moved on to what Kate called "gesture drawing," where you're mostly looking at the subject rather than the page, and "blind contour drawing," where you look only at the plant, never look at the page, and never lift up your pencil.

As I had learned from spending ten years in the field watching Tina Thieme Brown draw illustrations for our Sugarloaf books, drawing is a way of *seeing*. Writing is certainly a way of seeing; I have observed plants very carefully for almost 40 years as I have described them for my nature books and articles. But as I had long suspected from watching Tina, drawing is a superior way of seeing. When you have to draw it, you really get into the nuances of leaf shape, venation, toothing, and flower structure. As I drew the plants growing next to the boardwalk, I felt fully immersed in the intricate details of their leaves and flowers.

So absorbed were Kate and I that we could not believe that more than two hours had passed since we'd sat down in the swamp to contemplate and draw our mystery flower. The flower's identity was still a mystery, but we knew a lot about it other than its name.

The rest of the outing was spent walking north on the boardwalk, into the deep shade of the silver maple swamp forest and then out onto my favorite rock outcrop facing the Georgetown waterfront. After basking in the view of the city (and with a few less than complimentary shared remarks about some of the waterfront architecture) we headed west and inland to the Roosevelt Memorial.

I asked Kate to read and ponder the stone tablet with TR's "Nature" quotes. She loved them all, but was as curious as I was about the last quote: "Conservation means Development as much as it does Protection," concluding, as I had, that context was necessary for a full understanding.

When we got back to the car, where the 7-pound *Flora of Virginia* was waiting, we tackled the tome's daunting botanical key and finally discovered the name of our plant—the marsh dewflower, which was indeed related to the Virginia dayflower— and the not-so-great news that it was indeed invasive. But the name and status of the plant seemed almost beside the point after the depth of the experience we'd had.

Chapter Four

October — Island Happy Hour

October 4th: Happy Hour at the Island

I have been prepping for a Smithsonian Associates lecture and all-day tour of Rock Creek Park, and so my focus has been on Rock Creek, not Theodore Roosevelt Island. My work takes me to many parts of the city and beyond, where I lead all sorts of trips and tours, weaving narratives from historical threads and my love of nature and natural beauty. I am deeply grateful for the ability to do work so close to my heart, but I often feel tension between what I've planned and scheduled and what I want to do in the moment. I've been itching to kayak around the island before the boathouses close for the winter. On my way home from an appointment in Fairfax, Virginia yesterday, I was determined to get out on the water.

Before leaving Fairfax, I set my GPS for Thompson Boat Center on the Foggy Bottom waterfront. I hadn't registered that my route would take me across the Theodore Roosevelt

Bridge on my return from northern Virginia, directly over the inlet between the main island and Little Island, summer home of the ospreys. As I neared the city, suddenly two curvaceous walls of green arose beneath me, surrounded by water, and I was heading out between the islands. What an enticing view, knowing that I would soon be on the water and paddling toward those island shores.

I hopped in a kayak at the Thompson dock and headed toward the islands on a sunny late afternoon. High-school crew teams were gathered on the dock and they would be out on the river during my trip. I brought little with me but my keys and license, and I tucked my phone beneath my life vest so that I wouldn't be tempted to make notes or take pictures. I felt a deep desire to use every moment between 4 and 6 p.m. for full communion with the river and shorelines with no distractions.

As soon as I crossed the Georgetown Channel of the Potomac, I was greeted by the Japanese pagoda tree we'd identified on our summer paddling trip. The dark green leaflets of the young tree were adorned with hanging lighter green segmented pods, like so many strands of the pop beads we played with as kids, and the tree was vertically entwined with the wine-red leaves of a Virginia creeper vine. The greens of pagoda tree leaf and pod and the red of the climbing vine comprised stunning contrasts, and I couldn't help admiring the aesthetics of this invasive tree. The reddening vines of Virginia creeper, with its sharply toothed palmately compound leaves—each with five leaflets—and the slightly duller wines and yellows of climbing poison-ivy vines, with their smooth-margined compound leaves of three leaflets, were the only signs of fall I'd see during my trip around the island.

The tide was lower than ever, with extensive gray-brown mudflats encircling the island that could have been at home on the coast of Maine. Rosh Hashanah had begun the previous evening so this was a new moon tide. I recalled that tides were especially low and high at both new and full moons. The not-so-felicitous side effect of the low tide was a nearly paddle-proof continuous green mat formed by the invasive aquatic plant *Hydrilla*, which circled most of the island. A disheartening flotilla of plastic bottles and polystyrene cups floated on top of it. However, there was a huge upside: the birds. Long-legged great blue herons were stationed all around the island, patiently standing and stalking as they engaged in their Zen-like quest for fish. Mallard ducks numbered in the dozens, but the big story was the wood ducks.

As I neared the Theodore Roosevelt Island Bridge overpass and paddled past my twentieth brilliantly plumed wood duck, I began to think that every wood duck in town was at the island for happy hour. The juveniles had matured since my summer visits, and the adult males were back in their breeding plumage. A male wood duck with his multicolored feathers bathed in lowering autumn sunlight is a sight to behold. The females were beautiful too with their more muted feathers and white eyeliner.

As I neared Little Island and kayaked under the big bridge, it was time to face the fact that the ospreys would not be there to greet me. And indeed, as I paddled around the tip of the smaller island, it was clear that they had headed south. I looked up to see dead and dying green ashes, with no ospreys boldly claiming the most dramatic treetops as they had since midsummer. The silence denoting their absence was palpable between the periodic zoom of ascending and descending planes.

Their migration is stirring up uncertainty for me, and feelings of vulnerability. How many years into the future will ospreys leave Theodore Roosevelt Island and Little Island in the fall and return in the spring? Will the rising waters of the Chesapeake Bay and tidal Potomac eventually submerge parts of these islands? When? In 50 years? 100? That's not such a long time from now. I first stepped foot on Theodore Roosevelt Island nearly 40 years ago. Roosevelt was still alive 100 years ago.

It is so hard for us to think ahead for even one human lifetime when it comes to pondering protective action on climate change. I can't help but think that Roosevelt, had he known what we know now, would have had foresight and acted upon it. Our twenty-sixth president understood that a society that didn't protect its resources invited an impoverished future. And he was a fearless trust-buster, unafraid to challenge corporate interests when they conflicted with the common good. Aren't these the leadership qualities we cry out for now?

Roosevelt said: "I recognize the right and duty of this generation to develop and use the natural resources of our land; but I do not recognize the right to waste them, or to rob, by wasteful use, the generations that come after us."[13] A little digging taught me that this is the line that followed the mystery phrase on the nature tablet: "Conservation means Development as much as it does Protection." Roosevelt included the lines in a speech given in Kansas.

As I paddled past the inlet between the islands and the extensive mudflats that prevented my entering the inlet, where two great blue herons were gainfully employed, my sad human heart was lifted up by a joyful sound. A kingfisher, chattering away, was dipping and gliding between the islands. The bird landed in a dead ash tree along the nearby shore of Theodore Roosevelt Island and began scanning the waters below her for fish. This was the first time I'd seen a kingfisher at the island since my initial encounter in July.

How kind and savvy of her to come along and fill the void, shutting down my gloomy musings with her vivid life! For a time, she flew in front of my boat, beneath and beyond the western span of the Theodore Roosevelt Bridge. When she landed in another dead ash, I saw the rusty belly band identifying her as a female. I began to wonder: Could she be the very same kingfisher? I hope she'll fly with me again before approaching winter beaches the kayak fleet.

October 17th: Whitehurst Woman

Before setting up my laptop on the picnic table in our backyard, I had to brush aside a little pile of chewed-up acorn shells. The squirrels and other animals and birds are having a field day this fall with the abundant acorn crop. When winds at the outer edges of Hurricane Matthew grazed our city earlier this month, the rooftops rang with bouncing acorns.

After several days of real fall weather, it is warm again this afternoon. I'm sitting in the backyard barefoot, nursing a ginger-flavored Kombucha drink. My first white-throated sparrow of the fall sang from our oak tree this morning as I was lazing in bed. I had just read an account of the white-throated sparrow sweetly singing in the Adirondacks written by a young ornithologist named Theodore Roosevelt. This sparrow nests in the Northeast, where our extended family lives, but comes back to spend each winter here with us. I hear its dulcet tones from fall through early spring, and then it flies north in late April or early May, just at the time the wood thrush returns from the neotropics to sing his arias in Rock Creek Park. As one songster departs for the north, another arrives from the south.

Warm weather following crisp autumn days is often called "Indian Summer." I hope this phrase honors the Indians, who must have taken advantage of the balmy bonus days to lay up food stores for the winter. But I fear it's related to the phrase "Indian Giver," one of the most cruelly ironic labels ever, considering that those who use it are descendants of people who reneged on every treaty with this land's first people.

This is the sort of labeling that our current Republican nominee for president uses. His opponents are "liars," "incompetents," and "abusers," labels that he might think about turning on himself. He is fanning the flames of racism in this country with turnabout tactics that he frequently aims at minority groups. Oh gosh, why go there on this lovely late afternoon of autumn crickets and golden light?

I have not been back to the island since my last account, but I have gazed upon its shores longingly from across the wide Potomac, most notably during the bus tour I led for 40 people sponsored by Smithsonian Associates. This was one of the most ambitious tours I've ever led in scope and duration. We followed Rock Creek from its mouth across from Theodore Roosevelt Island to the northern border of the national park at the DC/ Maryland line. The tour was seven hours in duration and I used a microphone the whole time, dispensing historical tidbits and natural history both on the bus as we rode along the Rock Creek Parkway and Beach Drive, and off the bus as we explored historic sites and woodland trails.

Rebecca Roberts of the Smithsonian Associates (a journalist herself and daughter of journalists Cokie and Steve Roberts and granddaughter of House Majority Leader Hale Boggs and Congress member Lindy Boggs) invited me to do the tour and planned it with me. She met me at the mouth of Rock Creek in her tall rubber puddle-stomper boots last spring and agreed that this was the place for us to begin the foray. We mapped out the itinerary together that day and then it was up to me to fill in details. And what an adventure this became!

By the time Rebecca and I led our large group off the bus and on foot over the southernmost footbridge crossing Rock Creek, past the docks of Thompson Boat Center, and over to the mouth of the creek, I had consulted an archeologist, geologist, three historians, a National Park Service Ranger at Great Falls, several books, websites, maps, and tide charts. And that was just for my research on the mouth of the creek. Add on the historians, miller, biologists, water-quality experts, and others I consulted for the rest of the journey through the park, and I was so steeped in the lore of Rock Creek that I dreamed about it night after night.

At the start of our tour, we looked out over the wide Potomac toward Theodore Roosevelt Island, our backs to the mouth of Rock Creek. I showed them where the rocky rolling Piedmont gave way to the flat sandy Coastal Plain on the island, as geologist Joe Marx has taught me, in the vicinity of the Theodore Roosevelt Bridge. Rocky outcrops of the metamorphic Sykesville Formation were visible on the northern side of the island in our right-hand field of vision and then the tree-lined shore flattened out toward and beyond the bridge to the south and our left. As Joe has explained to me, much of the eastern portion of the island, upon which we gazed, is much younger than the main portion of the island to the north and west, having formed from sediments washed down the river from farms and overflow due to the levee and causeway built across Little River at the turn of the nineteenth century, impeding the river's flow on the western side of the island. The river was dredged during the 1920s and 1930s, according to Joe, and some of the sediments were piled on the eastern side, stabilizing the low-lying parts of the island.

As we gazed at the island, a sandy beach at our feet was visibly giving way to the Potomac's rising tide. Three major DC bridges were visible. The Theodore Roosevelt Bridge's decidedly utilitarian profile was bracketed upriver and down by the graceful curving architectural supports of Key Bridge to the north and Memorial Bridge to the south. Cars hummed over the bridges, and planes and helicopters noisily cruised overhead. As I have been doing in my own heart and mind, I tried to frame the scene for our group as a power spot fueling our dynamic city with incoming and outgoing energy.

I then asked them to turn around to face Rock Creek and the large mounted Rock Creek watershed map that Rebecca had gamely carried from the bus. I showed them on the map how the main stem of the creek originated some 33 miles upstream with springs on and around the Laytonsville Golf Course. It then gathered energy from numerous tributaries draining a 77.4 square mile watershed, a watershed traversing suburb and city and gathering all manner of pollutants and sediment racing across their impervious surfaces along the way. I told them, as Joe Marx had explained to me: "If the mouth of Rock Creek weren't carrying a heavy sediment load, you could look down and see it cutting a deep channel through the easternmost edge of Piedmont bedrock."

They enjoyed hearing that I had traveled the full 33-mile length of the main stem of Rock Creek, on foot and by bicycle and canoe, and I loved reminding myself that my present-day explorations of Theodore Roosevelt Island were a natural and logical extension of the journey, although it took a kingfisher who may have covered some of the same territory to point it out to me.

After framing the present-day scene, I started taking the group back in time, beginning with the lore associated with the Watergate Hotel, looming above us, scene of the infamous 1972 break-in that eventually brought down the Nixon administration. I pointed out the Kennedy Center, immediately downriver.

I gave a brief history of the C&O Canal and towpath: "Canal mules transported cargo, making their slow way along the towpath, until 1924."

"Rock Creek served as the first stretch of the canal," I said, pointing out Milepost Zero in front of us.

"You can now start here on foot or bicycle," I continued, "and travel all the way to Pittsburgh on the 184.5-mile towpath and the connecting 150-mile Great Allegheny Passage Trail," adding, "That's where my daughter Sophie lives."

It was a buoyant energetic group, and I think some of them were envisioning hopping on a bike at that very moment and setting out for Pittsburgh.

I explained that the fall zone was critical in locating the tobacco port of Georgetown, and later the nation's capital, at this precise spot, near the last navigable point along the Potomac River, a reality that the C&O Canal attempted to circumvent with a water route and locks to contend with topographic challenges.

I said: "George Washington had tried to get around Great

Falls and other navigation obstacles by creating a series of skirting canals in his attempts to create a navigation and trade route from the Potomac to the Ohio years before ground was broken for the C&O Canal by John Quincy Adams in 1828, on July 4th. Remnants of Washington's Patowmack Canal are still visible today on the Virginia side of the river."

"Just as the fall zone determined the location of Washington and other East Coast cities," I went on, "it was also a topographic landmark for Native American tribes who traveled, traded, and lived along the Potomac and other eastern rivers for millennia. A canoe couldn't get over Great Falls any more than a ship could, although it could much more easily be carried around it. The base of the falls was an important fishing spot for Native Americans as fish pooled there during spring migration. Our Washington region became a major trading spot for tribes living along the Potomac and Anacostia Rivers."

As Frederick Gutheim noted in his 1949 classic *The Potomac*:

The very name Potomac in the Algonkin tongue is a verbal noun meaning "something brought," and as a designation for a place, "where something is brought," or, more freely, "trading place." Living as they did, on one of the great natural trade routes east and west through the mountains, north and south along the fall line, and with a highly developed and specialized culture, it was inevitable that the natives of this section should be great traders.[14]

Native peoples may have begun traveling up Rock Creek to hunt, fish, and forage as early as during the last Ice Age some 13,000 years ago. We know they have lived in this area since that time, when mastodons and mammoths roamed the land. Archeologists have uncovered Indian quarries, spear points, and other artifacts that date back at least 4,000 years. As I shared this background with the Smithsonian group I was building up to the big reveal: the tale of "Whitehurst Woman."

I learned about Whitehurst Woman from Scott Einberger's description of a 1990s archeological find in his book, *The History of Rock Creek Park*. I researched the discovery further for my Smithsonian tour, consulting DC's official archeologist Dr. Ruth Trocolli, who led me to helpful websites and a 2013 book that I had somehow missed, titled: *Bold, Rocky, and Picturesque: The Archeology and History of Rock Creek Park*. While standing next to the mouth of Rock Creek with the Smithsonian group, I read directly from the book, about the find that occurred practically within spitting distance of where we were standing:

Here the archeologists uncovered a pit that they named Feature 283, an unremarkable name for probably the most important Native American find yet made in the District of Columbia. Feature 283 was a burial containing the remains of an adult, probably a 30- to 40-year-old woman. She had been cremated elsewhere, and then her scattered bone fragments were placed in a shallow pit measuring about 2.3 feet in diameter. Along with the bones were a comb carved from antler; two stone pendants, one slate, one schist, each with a single drilled hole; a carved sandstone phallus; a triangular knife of black chert; 14 great white shark teeth, 12 fossilized and two apparently recent; a bone from a large bird; six antler disks; a wooden bead; and textiles woven of fibers from pawpaw and some kind of grassy plant...Radiocarbon dates put this burial at AD 640 to 790 [some 1,300 years ago]. Most of the artifacts closely resemble objects found in graves in what we call the Kipp Island phase of central New York, part of a culture that stretched from the Great Lakes to the Delmarva Peninsula. Similar artifacts were found at the Island Field Site in Delaware.[15]

As Scott noted in his book, and as I pointed out to the group assembled at the mouth of the creek, this woman was probably revered as someone of high status in her tribe. In the days since my paddle up Rock Creek and my Smithsonian tour—as we are poised to elect either the first woman president in US history three weeks from tomorrow *or* a beauty pageant owner and playboy who rates women according to their looks on a scale of one to ten and was revealed bragging about sexual assault on a recently released video tape—I can't help but contemplate the irony of how regressively women are often treated in our culture, in contrast to how highly they were regarded by the Native Americans who preceded us with their own democratic societies. Our democracy, which we claim to have modeled on that of Classical Greece, is actually modeled more on Native American governments than we care to admit. However, like the Greeks of the Classical period in Athens, we denied women the vote for well over a hundred years, and former slaves for nearly as long.

As I continue to spend as much time as possible at Theodore Roosevelt Island, in Rock Creek Park, and other green spaces with which DC is still so blessed, I can't help but contemplate the related bitter irony of how we treat the land in comparison to its first human inhabitants. I think we are finally coming around to the knowledge that we have to learn to tread more lightly, although I'm not sure the Republican presidential candidate shares that view.

The dominant culture is far removed from the wisdom of our Native American predecessors and their descendants. Descendants like Donna House, an ethnobotanist of Dine'/ Oneida origin, who chose the plants to landscape the Smithsonian Museum of the American Indian, which opened in September of 2004 with a grand procession of tens of thousands of native peoples on the Mall. Before choosing plantings for the grounds of the museum, Donna House spent time canoeing on the Potomac River. Later she explained that she canoed the Potomac and explored the museum grounds "to let the landscape know I was there and to acknowledge all the different plants and animals who live around us."[16]

October 18th: Another Happy Hour—Hot Yet Autumnal

The voice of Nobel laureate Bob Dylan, christened as such just days earlier, was blasting from the speakers at the Key Bridge Boathouse in his original rendition of "Forever Young" as I stepped into a kayak on a Wednesday afternoon—a day of summer temperatures and autumn colors. As I paddled out toward a middle arch of Key Bridge, The Grateful Dead's "Ripple" came over the airwaves. I smiled to myself, slightly smug in the knowledge that young people are still listening to songs released when I was their age.

As I approached the island from the north, several gulls were soaring above the river in the warm air currents. I was grateful for the grace of the gulls with the ospreys off to their winter quarters.

As the island's profile came near, I saw that although the weather app on my phone said 86 degrees Fahrenheit (30C), the shoreline spoke: *Autumn*. Golden elms, bright yellow hickories, and the still-living golden ash crowns were accented by vivid wine-red climbing vines of Virginia creeper. The island woods were like a great golden package tied with vertical red ribbon. Paddling close to the shore I came upon a fallen tree with a bevy of mallards lined up boy–girl–boy–girl all along the trunk. Some were standing on orange legs and some were sleeping with bellies snug to bark and heads tucked in feathers. In the water around them their friends and neighbors were diving, preening, and quacking.

How could anyone feel depressed while watching ducks, I thought, as I have thought many times in the past. There is something so warmly communal and inherently optimistic about a gathering of ducks. Their paddling, quacking, and preening always uplift my spirits. Perennial note to self: Should blues come on, seek ducks.

As I made my way down the eastern shore of the island, I saw no wood ducks, only mallards. Apparently, the happy hour clientele is malleable (no pun intended). Midway down the shoreline I saw one of the island's great blue herons catch a small wriggling fish. Rather clumsily the heron dropped his catch, which was quickly recovered from the shallow water and hastily swallowed, heron dignity restored.

The river was a dark autumnal mirror as I paddled south on the windless afternoon. Autumn leaves floated on the surface of the water and over the *Hydrilla* mats. The orange and brown leaves of elm, and sycamore, and the golden leaflets of boxelder, ash, and hickory barely moved on the surface of the outgoing tide and slow southern current, so unlike Rock Creek, where fallen leaves travel swiftly along. The contemporary, rectangular profile of the Kennedy Center, the classically columned Lincoln Memorial, and the towering obelisk of the Washington Monument all sparkled in the afternoon sun, and I saw the occasional large orange lollipop of a blazing sugar maple planted along the shore.

I came upon a large family of newly hatched, fluffy golden ducklings and their mallard mama about halfway down the island. My own maternal heart worriedly wondered if this late brood had enough time to mature before winter.

As I neared the Theodore Roosevelt Bridge, I could almost see through the partially bare shoreline trees and into the swamp. Passing under the bridge, I paddled past Little Island, still devoid of ospreys, and noticed what I've come to call "Shag Island" located mid-river between Little Island and the Memorial Bridge. This rock outcrop, sort of an oddity at the beginning of the Coastal Plain, is frequently replete with sunning cormorants, as it was on this day. These gawky-looking large black diving birds with bare golden skin around their bills often perch with wings outstretched in order to dry them. While some were sitting with wings spread and some merely sunning themselves, their friends and relations were swimming and diving around the little island.

The "Shag" part of the name christening comes from my maternal grandfather, Merton Crosby. My grandfather worked for the Army Corps of Engineers, tending to a large dam on the Pemigewasset River in New Hampshire, where he contracted a fatal case of lung cancer after many years of spraying a now-banned pesticide. My grandparents were both born in Maine, and after his retirement he and my grandmother, Amelia Crosby, moved back to their home state, where he only had a short time to live.

When we visited my grandparents during their retirement, my dad, a lifelong birder, often used my grandmother's telescope (which she employed to keep track of neighbors across the millpond in their Down East village of Whiting) for bird watching. Cormorants were among the population, and they were locally known as "shags," a term my grandfather used more loosely to apply to any big bird. Incredulous that my dad would waste his time looking at birds, my grandfather would intone, with amused disgust, "A shag's a shag!" This quickly became a family catchphrase.

Leaving the vicinity of Shag Island and paddling around Little Island, I saw another giant orange lollipop of a planted sugar maple along the Virginia shore. I also noticed a rather large body of water flowing into the Potomac from Virginia, which I later identified as the Boundary Channel. Gazing back toward the inlet between Little and Theodore Islands, I saw two more great blue herons. And then I got a big surprise.

Just after I kayaked under the Theodore Roosevelt Bridge I saw a large bird high up in a tall golden-crowned tree that was vertically wrapped with the red ribbon of Virginia creeper. I paddled closer until I could make out the pale breast, dark eye-stripe, and slightly pointed crest of an osprey.

There was one still here!

Stephanie Mason, senior naturalist for the Audubon Naturalist Society, told me later: "The young-of-the-year are the last to head south. And while their elders travel all the way to South America, young osprey may go only partway." She added: "Wherever they end up, the young osprey will spend 18 months developing their hunting savvy before returning north to establish their annual adult migration."

How could it be that birds I'd watched diving and fishing, and heard keening all summer, travel ten times as far as most of the planes taking off from National Airport each autumn? And then, with no radar equipment or control tower, return to this island in the Potomac the following year? Ornithologists theorize that birds migrate extraordinary distances to precise destinations using some combination of the Earth's electromagnetic energy, the compasses of sun and stars, and even, perhaps, olfactory information. In recent years tiny solar-powered transmitters have been strapped to the backs of ospreys to track their whereabouts. According to Cornell University's "All About Birds" website, in 2008 a female osprey left Martha's Vineyard Island in Massachusetts and flew alone for 2,700 miles to French Guiana in 13 days.

Ospreys live on every continent but Antarctica and they mate for life. Imagine keeping a relationship intact while traveling the globe twice a year.

The western shores of Theodore Roosevelt Island where the osprey was perched were dazzling in the afternoon sun—the hickories, black walnuts, American elms, living ashes, boxelders, and maples all lit up with the full autumn palette. The large sycamores were showing off the glamor of their whitened upper limbs through their golden crowns. Many trees, including the silver maples, were still green.

The view upriver toward Key Bridge was a handsome sight,

the gray stone towers of Georgetown University rising above the green and white Potomac Boat Club and the silver-green Washington Canoe Club. Beyond the bridge, a full lush tree canopy bracketed both sides of the Potomac. Peeking in to the Theodore Roosevelt Island trails, I could make out high-school cross-country teams streaking through the woods in their colorful running clothes. Rounding the northern edge of the island, I saw that crew teams were out in force on the river, sleekly traveling north. Planes streaked overhead, and cars, walkers, and cyclists traveled over the high arches of Key Bridge. The river flowed, the tide ebbed, and autumn leaves drifted slowly along the shining river surface. As I dipped my paddle in the river, a chattering kingfisher flew in front of me, headed toward the Virginia shore, and I thought, *This* is the city that I know: commuters heading home, rowers heading upriver, tide going out, river flowing, planes flying. *This* city, not the gridlocked city of partisan rancor on a hill that the world often views with scorn. Everything flowing gracefully in all directions with one cautious juvenile osprey still clinging to the crown of an island tree.

Chapter Five

November — The Kingfisher Court

November 4th: The One Indispensable Requisite

Yesterday my parents celebrated their sixty-fifth wedding anniversary in Hanover, New Hampshire, where they have lived for many years. They were married in a chapel at the Marine Corps base at Quantico, where my dad, a 23-year-old marine, was stationed, and they honeymooned at the Willard Hotel in DC. During their time here, my 21-year-old mother rode a segregated bus from Alexandria to and from her job as a nurse at DC's Children's Hospital. All my life she has told stories about how the black children were treated in the hospital at that time. She said they were separated from their parents before tonsillectomies, a frightening thing for a child, while the white children were allowed to stay with their parents before their procedures.

My mom is now suffering from some debilitating form of dementia, probably Alzheimer's, and severe hearing loss. My dad still plays golf and tennis, works out at the Dartmouth College gym, and skis black diamond trails. On his eighty-eighth birthday in March he emailed me: "I took my skis to the basement this morning and brought my golf clubs up." He gave up ice hockey a few years ago. Despite his active athletic schedule, most of his time and energy are devoted to taking care of my mom, who still lives at home and finds joy in life, especially when she is with my dad, her children, grandchildren, and great-grandchildren.

My dad gave her a card for their anniversary that included the lyrics to a Nat King Cole song that one of their friends spontaneously sang to them at their wedding reception. The song, "Too Young," describes a couple who know their love will last despite the world's skepticism, firm in the belief that someday the world will acknowledge what they know.

Yesterday I had the joy and privilege of spending the morning on Theodore Roosevelt Island with two extraordinary women who are themselves the granddaughters of extraordinary women. Joanna Sturm's grandmother was Alice Roosevelt Longworth, the intrepid, outspoken firstborn child of Theodore Roosevelt. Kristie Miller's grandmother was Ruth Hanna McCormick, member of Congress from Illinois, and a leader of the women's suffrage movement. Kristie has written biographies of her grandmother, and more recently of Ellen and Edith Wilson, the two wives of Woodrow Wilson. After Ellen died, Woodrow courted Edith in Rock Creek Park. Kristie's grandmother Ruth died when Kristie was three weeks old, but both women enjoyed a long, loving, and colorful relationship with Alice.

Both Joanna and Kristie are nature lovers. I met them in the middle of the footbridge to the island on a warm cloudy morning of vivid fall color, the golds still gold, the red leaflets of Virginia creeper and the orange and yellow of poison-ivy vines still beribboning the trees along the shore. Joanna had her binoculars around her neck, and Kristie had a book in her hands to present to me: *The Naturalist*, a wonderful book about Roosevelt by Darrin Lunde of the Smithsonian's National Museum of Natural History. I had already begun reading the book since Kate had alerted me to its existence on our journaling trip to the island. Tucked inside the book were some excerpts from *The Letters of Theodore Roosevelt*. The more I read, the more I appreciate Roosevelt's eloquence as a writer. My friend, the acclaimed Jefferson and Roosevelt scholar Clay Jenkinson, who has been prominently featured in several Ken Burns documentaries, calls Theodore Roosevelt the "readingest and writingest" of all American presidents. Clay is the founder of the Theodore Roosevelt Center at Dickinson State University, where the most extensive, and very user-friendly, Roosevelt archives are housed.

When Roosevelt was a young man in the Adirondacks, he wrote of the white-throated sparrow: "It has a singularly sweet and plaintive song, uttered with clear, whistling notes; it sings all day long especially if the weather be cloudy..."[17] Once we'd crossed the bridge, Joanna, Kristie, and I were poring over the large map that greets island visitors. As we considered which trails to take, a white-throated sparrow in the trees nearby sang that "sweet and plaintive song" that has been described as "old Sam Peabody Peabody Peabody" in New England and "oh sweet Canada Canada Canada" north of the border.

Then we fell into the multitasking at which women naturalists are so adept. Scanning the woods for interesting trees and their fall fruits and winter buds, always on the lookout for birds, stopping often to interrupt with naturalist observations, and yet simultaneously pursuing conversational threads that are easily broken by nature's wonders and then just as easily revived.

The main conversational current pervading this walk was serious in nature. As we three women walked, we were aware that we stood on history's knife edge. In five days, we would either elect our first woman president in the history of the United States, a former first lady, senator, and secretary of state who shared our views on a number of issues, or we would elect the real-estate mogul, Donald Trump. The choice could not be more stark, a choice that has forced America to face her deep divisiveness and the misogyny, racism, and disregard for the well-being of the Earth that underlie so many of our institutions and beliefs. In discussing the misogyny that pervades our culture and has aimed its laser beam at Hillary, we spoke of Eleanor Roosevelt and the hatred she endured when she stepped beyond the role of helpmeet to her husband, Franklin. Eleanor was Theodore's niece, his brother's daughter, as well as the wife of her distant cousin, Franklin Roosevelt.

As we approached the Theodore Roosevelt Bridge, my companions began reminiscing about its dedication, which they had attended as 18-year-olds with Joanna's grandmother, an event which briefly halted the young women's planned trip out west. Since they had been at the dedication, I chose a route that would take us under the bridge, and I showed them where the Canada geese and mallard ducks snooze under its overpass on hot summer days.

"I was also at the dedication of the Roosevelt statue with my grandmother," Joanna said. We would see the statue later during the walk.

"May I ask what your grandmother thought of her father's statue?" I asked.

"Oh, she hated it," said Joanna, "and she mumbled about it all during the dedication."

We walked under the bridge, through the invasive Japanese stilt grass and a few native wild oats, to the lookout over the inlet between Theodore Roosevelt Island and Little Island. The tide was well up, and I was disappointed to see no herons fishing and no wood ducks. Retracing our steps back under the bridge, I showed them my *feng shui* silver maple. They loved the tree and my take on its function as guardian of the island forest and protector from traffic malevolence.

They urged me to share my offbeat perceptions more freely, and I told them that spending time with them was sure to give me the courage and inspiration to do so.

As we walked, we scratched and sniffed spicebush twigs and picked up and smelled fallen black walnuts in their fragrant green husks. Joanna asked me if I'd ever smelled a ponderosa pine and said that their bark smells like vanilla. I told her that Japanese researchers have studied the health benefits of inhaling air that's infused with conifer smells, showing it can boost the immune system.

We entered the magic world of the tidal marsh and the swamp where maples, hickories, elms, and oaks lined the boardwalk in all their muted late-autumn glory: burnt sienna, rust, brass, gold, and the occasional brilliant orange or yellow of a red or sugar maple. Out in the middle of the swamp, the deciduous needles of planted bald-cypresses were a deep russet color. Mallard ducks quacked and splashed in the inlet's rising tide.

We started down the boardwalk, admiring the view of the Kennedy Center, which was framed in the foreground by cattails and black willows that were gracefully letting go of their slender leaves.

"That's the way to see the Kennedy Center," I said, the stark outline of its white walls much improved by its palustral frame.

The leaves of the young pin oaks flanking the boardwalk were a surprisingly vivid orange. Their scientific name is *Quercus palustris*, the second part of the name—the "specific epithet"—referring to their swamp habitat. As we walked, we came upon New York ironweed in seed. The buff-colored pappus hairs attached to its seeds were subtended by overlapping involucral bracts or phyllaries that looked like tiny artichoke leaves (the artichoke is a member of the same daisy family). Where the hairs had already blown away, the open phyllaries looked like small open flowers resembling tiny dogwood blooms. Kristie and Joanna appreciated the far subtler beauty of the ironweed in seed, so different from the brilliant purple of its late-summer and early-autumn flowers.

I was happy to discover that a portion of the boardwalk that had been closed for construction during the summer had been reopened, allowing for close communion with the bald-cypresses and their encircling upright woody root projections known as "knees." The trees looked as comfortably at home in their swampy surroundings as cypresses in the Atchafalaya or Everglades. Kristie and Joanna had trouble believing they were planted, and so, originally, did I.

I told them: "The naturally occurring Battle Creek Cypress Swamp in Calvert County is less than 50 miles away, and remains of ancient cypress trees have been unearthed in DC during various construction projects."

I urged them to smell some of the crushed foliage of the deciduous needles — so delightful and probably healthful — and I asked, "Is it my imagination or do I detect a hint of vanilla?"

The cones, which smell like Christmas in Grandma's pantry, were still too tightly wound for proper sniffing. Next month.

As we headed back down the boardwalk, Kristie spotted a black rat snake climbing a tree, which we stopped to watch. As it made slow progress upward, we all admired its smooth looping travel and sleek black body.

During our walk I learned that Joanna has ridden her bike all the way from Pittsburgh to DC on the Great Allegheny Passage Trail and the towpath, the route that I just recently learned about during my Smithsonian research.

After a few trail twists and turns we found ourselves at the great impervious plaza over which a larger-but-slimmer-than-life Roosevelt presides with his arm upstretched.

We all became thoughtful as we read the quotations on the third tablet, titled "Youth." The last line about character particularly grabbed all of us in light of the choice our country faces next week: "Alike for the nation and the individual, the one indispensable requisite is character."[18]

Joanna told us how much Theodore Roosevelt admired his father, an accomplished, kind, and philanthropic man of good character, whose death while TR was at Harvard was devastating to him.

As we rested on one of the rock walls, our conversation returned to the upcoming election. We talked about the prevalence of misogyny in present-day cultures. When I explained my theory about its origins in male envy of reproductive power, Kristie urged me to take an old manuscript out of the drawer and get it published. The title of the book I wrote so many years ago is *Womb Envy*, and it explores a phenomenon that I believe underlies the economic, religious, political, and social repression of women.

I can only hope that the next time I walk with these extraordinary women, we will be celebrating the election of our first woman president.

November 10th: There Will Be No Celebration

There will be no such celebration. In the wee hours of yesterday morning, Donald J. Trump was declared President-Elect of the United States to the dismay and disbelief of more than half the voters and contrary to pre-election polls. He lost the popular vote to Hillary Clinton by more than two million votes but prevailed in the Electoral College with strong support from white America and the "Rust Belt," an economically stricken part of the previously industrial Midwest. His election was a shock to almost everyone, and it felt like a body blow to me.

My husband, Jim, was distraught, mostly on my behalf. He was not excited by either candidate but knew how important Hillary's election was to me, and voted for her. My daughter, Sophie, and I have been crying off and on for the past 36 hours.

She said that she and her Muslim taxi driver were both in tears during an airport drive.

Jim and I returned home from a trip to drought-stricken, wildfire-ringed Chattanooga last evening after taking a long and winding route through the mountains of southwestern Virginia, where I learned the terrible truth. We had been in Chattanooga for a colleague's retirement party. As I unpacked my laundry last night, I inhaled the lingering smell of the smoke from the forest fires that are consuming Tennessee's dry hills.

Donald Trump says he wants to "drain the swamp" in Washington. Even his metaphors are environmentally insensitive. A swamp is a precious wetland, giver of life. I'm sure Trump has drained more than a few actual swamps in his day as a golf course developer. He wants to bring back coal, the dirtiest of the fossil fuels, remove every environmental regulation he considers business-unfriendly, and tear up the Paris Climate Agreement.

I'm leading my annual fall tree-tour of the Capitol grounds for the US Botanic Garden (USBG) in two days. I was disheartened to see that the inaugural fence is already up around most of the western front of the Capitol, fencing off many of the historic trees that I highlight for people on these tours. That now seems painfully symbolic rather than just the inconvenience it appeared to be when I scouted for the tour last week. In addition to a Trump presidency, we will also have a Republican-controlled Congress and at least one conservative judge appointed to the Supreme Court and positions filled on many lower courts. I fear for the future of women's reproductive rights and marriage equality.

I am an optimist, but I feel sorely tested today and I am certainly not alone. The airwaves are filled with outpourings of anger and grief, and there were demonstrations in cities across America last night. As I write, the Obamas are welcoming the Trumps to the White House this morning. I cannot imagine how they must feel. For many years Trump was a prominent leader of the "birther" movement, questioning Barack Obama's American-born legitimacy, which many people regarded as a thinly veiled racist attack on our first black president.

Both Obamas have been fiery campaigners for Hillary over the past weeks, declaring her the most qualified person ever to run for the presidency. They have publicly denounced Trump as unfit for the office. And now they must smile, shake hands, and welcome to their home the man who has declared war on nearly every Obama initiative. In the interest of the peaceful democratic transferal of power, they must do this gracefully.

Yesterday, Jim and I woke up both to the stunning political news and also to the beauty of the mountains of southwestern Virginia. We listened to Hillary's concession speech on my media device (an earbud apiece) as we walked the Virginia Creeper Trail, a scenic trail following an old railroad bed through the shale and limestone forested hillsides and over streams and sycamore-lined rivers. Maples held onto their last red, orange, and yellow leaves, and a few yellow leaves fluttered on the twigs of the slippery elms along the trail.

When Hillary concluded her speech, and reality fully hit, I broke into wailing sobs and then angrily shouted: "This country will never accept a woman president!" I stumbled across a trestle bridge and back toward our car in angry tears as Jim followed me down the trail, futilely trying to offer comfort.

When we were in Chattanooga, I had walked along the actual Trail of Tears, a stabbing historic reminder of the cruel nineteenth-century relocation of thousands of southeastern Native Americans, many of whom died along the route west across the Mississippi, in one of the darkest chapters in American history. Our history is filled with the light and the dark. I wish I could shake the feeling that we have just chosen the dark.

November 15th: The Sun and the Moon

The Friday night after the election, I dreamed the sun burned out. At first it shrank down to the size and shape of a hockey puck that you could hold in your hand. It turned gray, and slowly and sputteringly lost all light. Then we were offered a backup star to replace the sun, but it too shrank, turned gray, and died.

At that moment we all became disembodied and went whooshing off into space. It was a pleasing sensation to fly off into the universe. Later a group of visually transparent, semi-embodied women gathered in a room in space. While we connected and shared experiences, we heard a rumor that the men were off having an orgy in another room.

When I awoke from the dream and checked the news on my smartphone, I learned that the nearly full moon would come closer to Earth than it had all during my lifetime. Not since 1948 had the moon been this close. As I drove to Rock Creek Park Sunday evening to meet my friend Cris Fleming for a walk, the moon rose in front of me at the crest of Connecticut Avenue and East-West Highway, a pale gold orb larger than any rising moon I'd ever seen. Cris and I walked in the dark, watching the moon shine through the newly bare trees and shimmer as it was reflected in Rock Creek. The vision of the moon was bright, but our conversational threads were dark as we pondered our uncertain future.

Yesterday I stood on the southern shore of Theodore Roosevelt Island looking out toward Little Island with a band of new friends who are birders and environmentalists. The tide was even lower than at Rosh Hashanah and it almost looked as if we could walk across the mudflats to the smaller island. One little pied-billed grebe slowly swam in the river beyond the mudflats.

I could feel the pull of the moon as I stood next to the tidal flats.

"Can you feel it?" I asked Tim Reed, one of our group of friends who was standing next to me.

"Oh yes," he said.

During the walk, the magic of nature enthralled us and helped to heal our shattered hearts. Most of us were new friends, but, bonded by our love of the natural world and the sudden threat to its well-being, I felt as if we had known each other forever. I showed them the fuzzy reddish flower buds of pawpaw, and the little paintbrush that is the leaf bud at the tip of the twig, through a hand lens with ten times magnification. We inhaled walnut husks, spicebush twigs, and bald-cypress needles and cones. We touched the bark of tall silver maples, basswoods, and bitternut hickories with reverence and awe. We hungrily drank the muted golds, rusts, and burgundies of the island trees, and the occasional bright orange or red of a sugar or red maple.

And they opened my eyes further to the world of birds. I made notes on my phone about the gulls: the ring-billed gulls we saw all around us and the lone great black-backed gull that Dave Sperling spotted from the footbridge to the island. Sharon Forsyth told me that herring gulls could also be seen here, their legs pink compared to the yellow of the mature ring-billeds (although she said the immature ring-billeds also have pink legs). Herring gulls are the ones most familiar to me from my childhood summers on Nantucket where they were always just a few feet away from our beach towels.

Looking out from under the Theodore Roosevelt Bridge to Virginia's Boundary Channel, we watched a great blue heron fishing and several wood ducks paddling near the mouth of the channel. The woodland trails were alive with the sights and sounds of small songbirds—chickadees, nuthatches, titmice, juncos, white-throated sparrows singing their plaintive songs, and their cousins the song and swamp sparrows. Carolina wrens loudly sang "teakettle teakettle teakettle" and darted about with their russet feathers and tiny upturned tails. We watched flickers and downy woodpeckers probe the bark of trees for food.

As we focused on the birds and all their antics, our heavy hearts lightened. There was nothing we could say to each other about the election that would uplift us. The birds did the lifting for us. I felt grateful to be in the company of birders, with their perceptive eyes and ears tuned to the avian activity in a world far from the political one.

As we stood on the boardwalk admiring the buff-colored pappus hairs and phyllaries of the New York ironweed and viewing the Kennedy Center through its cattail and black willow frame, a large bird wheeled into view above us: a magnificent bald eagle. Our national bird circled the skies above the swamp for some time before soaring toward Virginia.

Sharon had heard rumors of the island's Shumard oaks, so we all went to see them near the rock outcrop overlooking the Georgetown waterfront. While we stood under their drooping lower branches gazing out toward the river, a thrush landed on one of the rocks in front of us. The birders quickly identified him or her as a hermit thrush, the official state bird of Vermont and another bird (like the white-throated sparrow) that I hear singing in the New England woods in the summertime. Occasionally I think I spot one during the winter in Rock Creek Park. Theodore Roosevelt wrote of the hermit thrush: "Perhaps the sweetest music I have ever listened to was uttered by a hermit thrush."[19] Oh for a president who knows and loves that flute-like song!

Heading back toward the footbridge, past a yellow-flowered witch-hazel in full bloom, we heard the unmistakable rattling call of a kingfisher. Looking west toward Rosslyn, we watched the handsome bird make swift progress over the water toward the island, chattering away. Then another kingfisher came into view, and soon the two were flying in tandem. However, unlike other tandem flight I've observed, this was a hostile interaction. One of the birds seemed to harass the other, and we saw tiny blue feathers flying. We were all stunned, having never seen such aggressive kingfisher behavior before.

Betsy Lovejoy noted, "It's not mating season," and I wondered how they could be fighting over a whole big wide river. Has national strife reached the very kingfishers?

Before leaving the parking lot we all vowed to go out together again soon.

"We need a name for our little group," I said.

Without hesitation, Tim responded: "The Kingfisher Court."

Chapter Six

December — Surreal Solstice

December 13th: Kingfisher Court Reconvened

It's been nearly a month since I've had time to write about the island that now has a firm hold on my heart. In the meantime, Thanksgiving has come and gone, along with our two adult children, Sophie and Jesse, and Sophie's black cat, Balsam. Thankfully their return at Christmas isn't far off.

How to capture the gestalt of the times? My nature buddy, the snowy-haired protector, defender, and lover of Rock Creek Park and all planetary things green, Doug Barker, put it best when he wrote to me after the election: "I feel unmoored."

Unmoored is how so many of us feel. As the newly elected president convenes a cabinet of climate-change deniers, corporate tycoons, military generals, and people who want to scrap the missions of the very agencies they are being called to helm, we are in uncharted waters. And I can't bear to read about the gruesome news out of Syria this morning where women and children are caught in the brutal crossfire in Aleppo. For my part I just want to cling to the bedrock of Theodore Roosevelt Island and hang on for dear life until we get through wherever this political nightmare is taking us.

I long for the island by day, I dream of it by night, and yesterday I visited again with my fellow nature enthusiasts, the "Kingfisher Court," minus Tim. Yesterday, blonde blue-eyed Betsy, dark-haired, dark-eyed Sharon, and Dave, who was wearing a hat and whose hair I guess I haven't seen yet, and I all met in the parking lot and headed across the footbridge to the island. We were greeted by silver maples sporting bodacious red flower buds, the marcescent leaves of beech trees, and the groovy-barked basswoods with their decorative "bats and balls" hanging fruits.

Dave said, "Let's go left instead of right," after we'd crossed the bridge, adding, "We always go right."

Left it was, and we quickly applauded the decision as we were able to focus our freshest attention on the noteworthy trees of the floodplain forest: small but stalwart and sinewy musclewoods hugging the shoreline; tall cinnamon-barked river birches, their delicate twigs and winter catkins breezily dancing under the white sky; thick-barked black walnut trees, the ground around them adorned with half-eaten nuts. We passed a tall eastern cottonwood and a grove of osage-orange trees, with fallen grapefruit-sized fruits lying around as if in wait for the mastodons and mammoths with whom they may have co-evolved. We walked under an extremely tall tree of the red oak group that could be a Shumard (I will need outside botanical help with this one), and, on slightly higher ground, we saw shaggy-barked white oaks with brown-pink marcescent leaves still clinging to their twigs.

I led the group to a large riverside tree I've named "Grandmother Sycamore." During my summer paddling trips I fell for this ivory-barked tree clinging to an island rock of the metamorphic Sykesville Formation. As we were admiring the venerable exposed root system of the sycamore, Sharon spotted three pied-billed grebes in the river between us and the Rosslyn skyline. With feathers the exact buff color of ironweed pappus hairs, and short, stout bills, this adorable threesome regaled us with their diving antics, disappearing in tandem and then reappearing upriver. While we walked, a bald eagle flew overhead.

When the Kingfisher Court arrived at my favorite rock outcrop on the east side of the island and stood beneath the Shumard oaks, the cloud cover suddenly thinned and a golden sun shone through. As the day brightened, so did the bird life. A tiny ruby-crowned kinglet flitted from tree to tree, while a stately great blue heron stood on bedrock next to the water, silently preening his or her glorious gray neck feathers. We saw five species of woodpeckers—pileated, downy, hairy, red-bellied, and flicker—drawn to the dying ashes and their abundant insect life. White-crowned, song, and fox sparrows explored the leaf litter along the shoreline for food. The birders of the Kingfisher Court were especially excited to see a migrating fox sparrow, and so was I when I got a good look at the bright rufous streaks on the breast of a foraging bird and then noticed its pink legs as it flew into a tree.

Three goldfinches were dining on the small brown cone-like fruits of a smooth alder shrub growing from the rock outcrop near the river. Dusky pink catkins hung down from the outermost twigs, and the pale yellow of the birds against the pink catkins was aesthetically sweet.

Looking across the Potomac toward Thompson Boat Center, we saw many ring-billed gulls and one great black-backed gull near the mouth of Rock Creek.

As we turned around to head toward the boardwalk through the swamp, I spotted another native shrub I hadn't noticed previously. One shrub quickly became four as I widened my gaze: rather uncommon shore-loving bladdernuts, which I've seen upriver at Carderock, along Rock Creek, and on the western side of Theodore Roosevelt Island. I shook the limbs of one of the bladdernuts so that Betsy, Dave, and Sharon could hear the dry seeds rattling inside the hanging papery capsules ("nature's maracas," my naturalist friend Stephanie Mason calls them). Then I opened a capsule so they could see and hold the seeds, which look and feel like shiny popcorn kernels. We did this on a Rock Creek Park walk I led for the Rock Creek Conservancy earlier this month, a walk attended by staunch environmentalist and newly elected Congressman from my district in Maryland, Jamie Raskin, and his wife, (soon to be former) Deputy Secretary Sarah Bloom Raskin, the highest-ranking woman ever to serve in the Treasury Department.

A little later the Kingfisher Court came upon a majestic bitternut hickory growing near the silver maple forest at the northern end of the boardwalk. "Wow!" we all exclaimed as we trained our binoculars on its mustard-colored buds. Betsy found a fresh hickory nut on the ground, tucked within its protective husk. We each touched the four small winged seams on the surface of the husk that are characteristic of the bitternut hickory, a native floodplain tree.

Betsy, Dave, Sharon, and I followed a retreating flock of small gray and white juncos—winter residents of the island who were foraging in the cracks of the boardwalk—through the venerable silver maples and green-twigged boxelders. The female boxelders sported wheat-colored paired samaras, many of which had fallen onto the boardwalk, where they would soon become somebody's feast.

As the afternoon warmed, we looked up to see small white clouds flying across a now blue sky. Out of nowhere a delightful fragrance greeted us. We followed it to the bald-cypress grove, where the rusty-needled deciduous conifers sported their odd and lovable "knees." The fragrance arose from the cones, some still on the trees, and others lying amid the needle-blanketed knees and split open by animals or birds on the boardwalk. Whoever dined on them had released their spicy citrusy bouquet into the air, which we gratefully inhaled.

Sharon said that she had kept a cone I gave her on the last walk. She said she takes it out to inhale its fragrance whenever she feels low. Yes! I thought. We can't cure the political world just now, but we can inhale the fragrance of bald-cypress cones as we dream of better days.

As we breathed the cypress-infused air, a red-shouldered hawk flew past, with breast feathers the color of the clinging and fallen cypress needles. He or she landed in a tree across the tidal inlet.

After watching the hawk, we walked back to the main boardwalk, down past the ironweed with its flowery phyllaries, some still clinging to grebe-colored pappus hairs attached to lovely little seeds you could hold in your hand before the wind lifted them up and away. A string of small bead-like male cypress cones had been carried by the wind, landing on an ironweed plant. At the end of the boardwalk near the Theodore Roosevelt Bridge, male and female mallards were lined up and perched on a partially submerged log in the boy–girl fashion I'd so enjoyed on one of my early-fall kayaking trips. I shared my duck theory with my friends: It's hard to feel blue while watching ducks.

As we wandered out to the inlet between Theodore Roosevelt Island and Little Island, we noted how much the tide had come in during our walk. We'd lost all track of time. Someone checked and we'd been out for three hours.

I laughed and said, "Data will show that during the Trump years birders extended their walks by an average of one hour."

We walked out to a point of land with a view of hundreds of Canada geese in the shallow blue water. We quietly beheld the birds and the handsome Memorial Bridge beyond before returning to our daily routines and the news of the day.

December 15th: An Upriver Adventure

Yesterday my body and soul cried out for wild adventure on more challenging terrain than mostly flat Theodore Roosevelt Island or gently rolling Rock Creek Park. Sugarloaf Mountain seemed a little far afield. Casting about for ideas I had a sudden inspiration: the Billy Goat Trail.

This 2-mile trail on Bear Island in the Potomac Gorge, 15 miles upriver from Theodore Roosevelt Island, bears dire warnings at the outset and along challenging stretches of the trail. A sign at the trail's midpoint reads:

> Many hikers are injured every year on this section of the Billy Goat A trail. The terrain includes sharp drops, requires jumps across open areas, walking along the edges of rocks, and a climb up a 50-foot traverse…If you are tired, low on water, or unprepared for a very strenuous hike, please turn back.

I've only hiked the Billy Goat A Trail a handful of times and never alone, although I've led many nature walks on the less strenuous Billy Goat B, starting from the towpath near the climbing wall at Carderock. I've hiked Billy Goat A several times with Jim and twice with my son Jesse, once when he was 10 years old and again just a few weeks ago during Thanksgiving. When he was 10, we identified wildflowers springing from the rocks with Newcomb's wildflower key, and he proved to be an ace botanist. Last month, he revealed the graceful agility of a fit 25-year-old, and I was pleased to be able to keep up with him, however tardily.

Early yesterday afternoon I popped my bicycle in the back of Jim's truck and headed up to Great Falls. From there I biked the 2-plus miles to Old Angler's Inn, where I chained my bike to the railing of a footbridge traversing the C&O Canal towpath. The Billy Goat Trail departs from the towpath just above Old Angler's and rejoins the towpath just south of Great Falls.

Turning north from Old Angler's on foot, I reached the Billy Goat Trail entrance, where I found these words on a sign created by the Nature Conservancy and the National Park Service:

> This 15-mile section of the Potomac River, from Great Falls downstream to Theodore Roosevelt Island, is one of the most ecologically significant natural areas in the entire National Park System. Despite its proximity to the urban bustle of Washington, D.C., this corridor contains one of the highest concentrations of globally rare natural communities in the nation.

As I walked toward the dramatically rocky Potomac shoreline under an overcast sky, I marveled over the quiet of the scene. Apparently 15 miles is all it takes for a plane to fly so high aloft that it's a distant hum rather than the reverberating body buzz I experience downriver at Theodore Roosevelt Island, the southern end of the Potomac Gorge. The stillness of the trees accentuated the movement of the birds and the occasional approaching hiker. There were trees growing right up from the trail, their exposed roots entwined with bedrock. As I stepped over the rocks and roots, I held onto their trunks, as thousands, perhaps millions, of hikers had done before me. Each handhold was a direct communication with the beauty and stalwartness of the tree. Hackberry, American elm, musclewood, tulip-tree, Virginia pine, chestnut oak. I spoke their names to myself, in my mind, reverentially.

Asters and goldenrods bore small fuzzy clusters of pappus hairs attached to seeds just waiting for lift-off. Wild oats, bleached to a pinkish wheat color, lavishly lined the trail. I gently touched their thin, dry panicles as I walked. I thought about Amos Clifford, founder of the Association of Nature and Forest Therapy in California, and his desire to help people incorporate the forest and connect with their foraging ancestors through the simple act of drinking wild tea. When the forest was our livelihood—our source for food, shelter, warmth, and medicine—how much we treasured it! I thought about the word "treasure" both as a noun and a verb. *Treasure Island*, as I've silently been calling Theodore Roosevelt Island to myself, took on new meaning with "treasure" heard as a verb.

Fragments of Leonard Cohen songs flowed through my mind as I walked. Leonard died during the week of the election at the age of 82. After his death, and Trump's election, actress Kate McKinnon, who played Hillary Clinton on NBC's *Saturday Night Live*, sang an emotional rendition of his evocative song, "Hallelujah," on the show.

As the trail became more challenging, I thought primarily about where to put each foot and when to sink down and use upper-body strength to make it over the rocks. Last month, when I was trying to keep up with Jesse, I simply cruised along in the wake of his youthful energy and confidence. Alone, I quickly discovered that overthinking was as much of a danger as carelessness. Before stepping over a wide space and onto an angled rock, there was a sweet spot between no thought and too much thinking. I hadn't left myself much daylight, so I had to keep up a pretty good pace.

Partway along the trail, the rocks grow bigger and reveal delicious-looking caramel swirls. My geologist friend Tony Fleming wrote about these rocks in an email to me several years ago in answer to some questions I had before leading a field trip along the Billy Goat B trail:

The rock originally consisted of greywacke (impure sandstone) and mudstone that were deposited in a submarine fan at least 475 million years ago. When the Taconic volcanic arc collided with the east coast of North America during the Ordovician (circa 470–450 ma), these rocks were subsequently dragged into a subduction zone, severely deformed, and metamorphosed at high temperature (650–700 degrees C) and pressure (equivalent to 5–10+ miles depth), causing them to recrystallize and partially melt to form the veined rock known as migmatite.[20]

Tony, please forgive me for observing that the surface of the rock looks like pulled taffy.

As you climb on top of the massive gray and buff-colored migmatite outcrops (hopefully I'm back on *terra firma* here, linguistically speaking), you are suddenly looking at a gorge within a gorge, right into the deep channel of Mather Gorge, a geological youngster not much older than 30,000 years of age, lying within the much wider and longer Potomac Gorge. For no rational reason, staring into and across Mather Gorge makes me feel like I'm in the Himalayas or, even less rationally, on the moon. Mather Gorge definitely doesn't announce to the hiker: "I'm located just beyond the Beltway." As I stared into the aquamarine water flowing between two tall rock walls—one in Maryland and one in Virginia—I noticed a lone kayaker far below.

According to Tony, "the Mather Gorge Formation is classic *suspect terrain*, that is, it probably is not native to North America and was transported and accreted tectonically to the continent during the Paleozoic." He added:

The river is in a period of *strong downcutting*. Great Falls is now known to have initiated after about 37,000 years ago—it is only the most recent position of a falls that formerly stood at Black Pond, opposite the downstream end of Bear Island— so Mather Gorge was cut since then. As a result, most of the soil and weathered rock has been stripped off the walls of this part of the gorge, creating many large exposures of fresh bedrock and generally thin soils throughout the gorge area. Ledge communities are common in the area and feature plants well adapted to thin or no soil and growing out of crevices in rock outcrops. This type of environment features strong season swings in moisture availability, and commonly hosts dry-mesic forest types such as elfin pine-oak woods and shrub-heath glades.[21]

Indeed, I now found myself in the land of stunted oaks and venerable-looking yet petite Virginia or scrub pines. I admired the pines' evergreen needles in bundles of twos against the gray-white sky, and their hardy-looking and abundant egg-shaped cones. Blueberry and huckleberry plants, members of the indomitable heath family, sprang from crevices in the rocks. Walking was a challenging enterprise absorbing all my energies with little left to admire the aesthetics of the quietly dramatic scene.

Passing the midpoint, I climbed down a steep 50-foot wall and then up to an area of relatively smooth bedrock marked by intriguing potholes holding rainwater. I was approaching the land of bedrock terraces and depressional swamps, also described by Tony in his email to me:

> The terraces are composed of *alluvium*: sand, gravel, and mud deposited by the river when it flowed at terrace level. Although local rock fragments dominate the alluvium, it also contains much material derived from upstream, including limestone and dolomite from the Frederick Valley and Valley and Ridge sections. As a result, the alluvium is moderately calcareous, and creates a significantly richer environment for plants than bedrock outcrops.

I knew that the best examples of bedrock terraces were found on the Olmsted Island trail to Great Falls, which I wouldn't have enough daylight to explore, but have done so many times in the past. That's also the best place to see the depressional swamps, which Tony says are "fed by ground water seepage and precipitation, and have a strongly seasonal hydroperiod." He added that they "host some unusual wetland vegetation."[22]

Between Mather Gorge and Theodore Roosevelt Island, another type of rare habitat is found, which Tony described as *scour prairie*. Scour prairies are composed of rare and unusual plant communities that more closely resemble those of Midwestern prairies. Tony cited Chain Bridge Flats as the best "scour prairie" example. During the summer, while prepping for a wildflower trip, I had paddled north from Fletcher's Boathouse (about 2 miles north of Key Bridge) to the Chain Bridge Flats, where prairie plants grow, including big bluestem and little bluestem grasses. These grasses grow in the prairies of the Dakota badlands where a young Theodore Roosevelt cattle-ranched and hunted on and off for several years.

Dark was descending as I approached the northern entrance to the Billy Goat Trail. As I walked, I heard children's happy shrieks from across the river in Virginia. Just before reaching the towpath, I caught the unmistakable loud chatter of a fast-flying kingfisher. I ran as fast as I could to peek over a large outcrop to the Potomac below, but I didn't run fast enough to catch the bird in flight.

Walking along the towpath toward the Great Falls Tavern Visitor Center, I spotted an obligingly stationary avian friend: a great blue heron whom I had seen from my bicycle earlier in the afternoon. The lanky bird was wading in the canal waters on his or her quest for fish, while an industrious flock of male and female mallards paddled and foraged nearby. Just downstream, a small beaver dam made me smile as I looked about in vain for the construction crew.

As I recall yesterday's Billy Goat Trail adventure, I'm trying to distract myself from my last crazed wild hope: It's Thursday and the Electoral College doesn't vote until Monday.

Jim said to me in the wee hours of November 9th: "It's not

over until the Electoral College votes."

Electors have been flooded with requests to honor the nearly three million vote advantage of Hillary Clinton, coupled with Trump's lack of qualifications and Russian interference in the election. However, it's unlikely there will be more than a handful of defectors.

I'm listening to Beethoven's "Ode to Joy," the uplifting final movement of his Ninth Symphony, for comfort. My Sugarloaf area friend, Bev Thoms, urged me to listen to it after 9/11, and I felt a crying need for it today.

December 28th: The Longest Night

The Electoral College has voted, and the winter solstice and Christmas have passed. The sun is on its upswing journey in this hemisphere, but will the light return to our poor fractured country and our world? The Christmas season saw yet another terrorist truck attack on a festive holiday market in Berlin, killing at least a dozen people and injuring many others, and Aleppo has fallen after countless civilian deaths. In less than a month, Donald J. Trump, vindictive mad-tweeter, will be inaugurated as President of the United States. One of his latest tweets spoke of the need to increase our nuclear arsenal. There is no end to the terrifying lunacy.

From the mystical midwinter longest night, the pendulum swings us toward the longest day on the summer solstice. My Sugarloaf friends and I celebrated the solstice this year on Sugarloaf Mountain, as we did for the first time a quarter century ago. Now, we feel the need to gather and mark the year's shortest day and longest night more than ever.

So there we were a week ago today, on the afternoon of December 21st: 15 women, 1 man, and several dogs in a circle under the oak trees at West View on Sugarloaf, most of the children who celebrated with us years ago all grown up and flown away. When "Father Winter" passed the winter wand around our circle—a long stout stick decorated with the silver and blue ribbons we attached to it 25 years ago—we all shared our favorite aspects of the season. Each person offered something deep and eloquent about winter's beauty and its invitation for introspection.

Two days later, Sophie and Jesse arrived for our Christmas celebration. We decided to forgo our formerly lavish gift-giving this year so that we could give each other the greater gift of festive and unhurried time together. I decorated the house with greens and candles, Sophie and I made our traditional vegetarian holiday meal—manicotti—and we all had time to indulge in Christmas movies, long walks, and our favorite holiday songs including traditional Appalachian music by the Seeger family and raspy-voiced Bob Dylan's hilariously over-the-top Christmas album.

On Christmas Day in the afternoon we walked on Theodore Roosevelt Island, Sophie's and Jesse's first trip there. They found it a much more beautiful destination than they had envisioned. They delighted in the tall trees bearing their winter fruits and marcescent leaves and they simply loved the ivory-barked sycamores along the shore, with special reverence for Grandmother Sycamore. They were happily surprised to see so many other families out walking on a cloudy Christmas afternoon, many with adorable and friendly dogs. The tide was high and we saw no large birds other than Canada geese and ring-billed gulls, but the riverside views of the Lincoln Memorial, the Kennedy Center, and the Georgetown waterfront captivated Sophie and Jesse.

After circling the island, we paid a visit to the Roosevelt statue. They read many of the quotes on the tall stone tablets and found them inspiring. While our children explored the plaza in the waning sunlight, Jim and I sat quietly on a bench. From the surrounding trees, at first just one, then several, white-throated sparrows sang fragments of the song that Roosevelt described as "singularly sweet and plaintive."[23] The song felt like a direct communication from the nature-loving adventurer who had so appreciated the little bird with the powerful voice.

We had another musical experience last night: a Judy Collins concert at the Birchmere, a legendary venue for traditional music in Alexandria. Jim and I were there with our close friends Jim and Tina Brown. Judy had recorded her recently deceased friend Leonard Cohen's song, "Suzanne," to popular and critical acclaim when he was an obscure young poet. Judy is 77 years old and occasionally her voice cracks or she fails to hit the perfect note. However, when she sang "Suzanne" it was with the powerful voice of a young Judy Collins, and it put me in tears as I felt the certainty that Leonard was with us in the room, his spirit helping her to fluidly hit all the right notes with full feeling.

Earlier in the day Jesse and I had listened to the vinyl last recording that Leonard released a month before his death, my Christmas gift from Jesse: *You Want It Darker*. It is indeed dark, but we both instantly loved it, and as Jesse was packing his bags to return home to New York on the bus, he said, "This album rocks."

After hearing Judy Collins sing Leonard's "Suzanne," I remembered a dream I had two nights ago. I was floating down the Potomac River between Theodore Roosevelt Island and Alexandria, Virginia, on a raft at night. Every so often I would awaken and check the river and the shoreline to make sure all was safe for sleeping and drifting along. I would occasionally see other large objects drifting beside me in the river and I'd make out landmarks along the shore and assess them to make sure there was nothing threatening. When daylight came, I was somewhere between Alexandria and nearby Mount Vernon, and I woke up as I was trying to make out a way to climb safely ashore.

I attribute all of these tangentially connected fragments to the winter solstice, a time of spiritual yearning and deep dreaming of returning light. Our thoughts and dreams can get a little *surreal* this time of year, the word proclaimed by Merriam-Webster as 2016 "word of the year" and most searched on the internet. Theodore Roosevelt nearly lost his life on the River of Doubt, his darkest journey. This year, everything has taken on a surreal quality as we enter perilously unknown waters, our own River of Doubt.

Chapter Seven

January 2017—Withy Like the Willow

January 3rd: The New Year on the Island

I struggle to make New Year's celebrations meaningful. For me the winter solstice feels like the true new year, so what to make of this other new year's day, January First? Given that this new year would bring a troubling new resident to the White House, it was especially hard to feel celebratory. I didn't make it until midnight on the 31st, but I stayed up long enough to know that New Year's brought another act of terrorism, this time to a Turkish nightclub, where 39 people from many countries were killed in seven minutes.

On the last day of the year I tossed dried black-eyed peas, along with crushed tomatoes, green peppers, onions, and carrots, into the crockpot so we'd be able to eat them for good luck on New Year's Day, a pork-free adaptation of the southern "hoppin' John" tradition. When we lived in Comus and had a big garden (and a pet pig), we always saved some of our tender green black-eyed peas of summer in a dried state for New Year's Day. The story of the black-eyed pea as a lucky food goes back to the Civil War and the lore that Sherman's invading Union troops believed the peas were only suitable for animals, and thus left them behind when raiding southern food supplies. According to a story by Leada Gore that I found on an Alabama website:

> The "lucky" peas made their way to Southern tables, especially those of Southern slaves who celebrated emancipation as ordered by President Abraham Lincoln on January 1, 1863. After the war, peas were always eaten on the first day of January.[24]

The humble and lovely little black-eyed pea, family relation of the groundnut growing on Theodore Roosevelt Island, is celebrated in cuisines the world over. Like all edible legumes, the black-eyed pea is an economical and nourishing food and is, perhaps, my favorite of all of them. Certainly, it's the most adorable with its dark eye, which grows darker with drying. Sophie, Jim, and I had small bowls of our black-eyed peas with our breakfast.

Winter is the only time when our tap water runs really cold. Now that I'm spending so much time kayaking on the river in the summer, and gazing into its reflective surface year-round, I feel a newfound appreciation for our water source. What a privilege and a joy it is to have cold and hot running water from the Potomac River in our home! My first act on New Year's morning was to drink a tall glass of cold Potomac water straight from the tap. My next was to bathe in it, hot.

After breakfast, we said goodbye to Sophie who was returning to her home in Pittsburgh (Jesse had returned to Brooklyn a few days earlier), and Jim and I headed out to Theodore Roosevelt Island (following a midwinter's nap). We drove through Rock Creek Park, along the Georgetown–Foggy Bottom waterfront, around the Lincoln Memorial and over the Memorial Bridge to reach the island, singing along to the *Doors* 1967 album along the way (recently unearthed from our sprawling CD collection). For a long-married couple who will forever be children of the Sixties, the music helped ease the sadness and fill the void left by Sophie and Jesse's departures. Ever since I've known Jim, he has been singing and playing guitar, and when he's not singing, he's often humming, whistling, or drumming his fingers. I can't imagine life with Jim apart from music.

When we reached the island footbridge, two double-crested cormorants, one all-black adult and one juvenile with a paler breast, were swimming and diving just downriver from the bridge. Little River was as clear as glass, as smooth and reflective as I'd ever seen it. Ivory-white sycamores, including Grandmother, were showing off all along the western shoreline as we approached. When we got close to the island, the bodacious red flower buds of the silver maples leaning over both sides of the bridge looked precociously bloom-ready. The little round yellow-green flower buds of the fragrant spicebushes in the riparian understory also looked ready to burst.

We had decided sometime between our nap and *The Doors* that we would hike the Upland Trail for the first time in many years. We approached the trail from the plaza surrounding the giant statue of Roosevelt, which I've begun to make peace with, and even like. I couldn't resist stopping to read his quote about character on the "Youth" tablet: "Alike for the nation and the individual, the one indispensable requisite is character."[25] I attempted to quell my seething thoughts about character and the incoming president, and walked on.

The Upland Trail, a long north–south trail that forks toward the southern end and parallels and overlooks the Swamp Trail, traverses the highest part of the island, affording iconic views of the Kennedy Center, Lincoln Memorial, and Washington Monument. From this wooded trail you look right down into the swamp and tidal marsh, where the tide was ebbing on this

New Year's afternoon. The upland forest is composed of tall hickories, reaching for the clouds, their braided bark a visual joy, massive old northern red oaks with "ski track" bark and fluted bases, many American hollies, American beeches, and tulip-trees. Healthy-looking eastern hemlocks, interspersed with the deciduous trees, seemed so far to have dodged a damaging blow from the Asian woolly adelgid, which has killed hemlocks throughout the east.

When we reached what seemed to be the height of land after choosing the eastern (swamp-side) fork in the trail, I was attracted to an old black walnut springing from a rock outcrop. I suggested to Jim that we do a little exploring, a proposal always guaranteed to pique his enthusiastic interest. Black walnuts on high ground often suggest historic residences as they are far more common in the floodplain and they were often the first trees early settlers planted, for their wood, nuts, and the rich brown dye that could be extracted from the husks around the nuts. The tree also has medicinal properties that were known to resident Indians and passed on to European settlers. Perusing the height of land, I wondered aloud to Jim if this could be the setting for John Mason's estate. A few minutes later my surmise was confirmed by a wayside sign Jim located next to the western fork in the Upland Trail. The sign featured a picture captioned "Mason Mansion about 1900" and read:

> John Mason had an elegant summer home on the small rise you see behind the sign. From about 1792 to 1830 it was a center of Washington and Georgetown society. A few bricks are all that remain of its former splendor.

We quickly returned to the rocky rise and found some of the bricks. Then, heading back to the eastern fork of the Upland Trail, we found a second, even more massive, black walnut tree. On the ground all around it were *hundreds* of black walnuts, some half-eaten, some still intact in their shells, and quite a few within both their shells and their remaining outer husks, which were blackened with age. Picking up the nuts still in their husks and smelling them, we discovered that they held some of the fragrance of summer and fall, when they are bright lime green on the tree and then, for a time, on the ground.

Standing in the midst of the fallen walnuts under the large old tree with its thick, ridged purple-black bark, I felt transported to the past. There is a black walnut tree downriver at River Farm near Mount Vernon that is believed to date to George Washington's time. Could these island trees date to John Mason's slightly more recent time? And even if they don't, aren't they likely descendants of trees that were here in Mason's time? John's father, George Mason, authored the Commonwealth of Virginia document that was a template for our US Bill of Rights. Surrounded by the abundance of the Mason trees during this troubled time for our country, I felt their regenerative power.

I took a deep breath, knowing how far-fetched my thoughts were about to sound, as I said to Jim: "I sense the wild wisdom of these walnuts and their ancestry, and I feel their symbolic connection to inspirational ideas that uphold the common good." Jim loved this crazy perception. Another shared joy of being long-married—radical acceptance of one another's outlandish thoughts.

A second wayside sign awaited us along the trail, showing a graphic depiction of Theodore Roosevelt Island cultivated end to end. It was titled "The Mason Estate" and read:

In contrast to the island today, this 1818 map by Robert King portrays the island as one continuous garden rich in native and cultivated plants, flowers, and fruits and divided into an avenue planted with trees. The estate was the summer retreat for the family of John Mason.

It's so fascinating that today's relatively wild Theodore Roosevelt Island, former Nacotchtank home, underwent a period of intense cultivation during the Mason years, when it was a destination for Washington society. Frederick Law Olmsted Jr., working with the Civilian Conservation Corps in the 1930s, returned the island to a more natural habitat of woodland forest with the planting of more than 20,000 woody plants, including those that were towering over Jim and me in the uplands.

The Upland Trail connected with familiar trails, and we followed one under the Theodore Roosevelt Bridge toward the inlet between TRI and Little Island. Jim noticed a rock outcrop along the shore adjacent to the trail before the inlet and we both wandered out to it. It was a delightful last bit of bedrock before the land gives way to flatter Coastal Plain. With the tide at nearly its lowest point, we were able to traverse the mudflats to get out onto the rocks in the river. From here we saw an adorable diving duck. He was small and alert-looking, with a short stiff tail and the most deliberate and endearing dive. Diving into the New Year, I thought. The duck had bright white markings on his face on either side of his gray bill. A quick check of the Cornell ornithology site on my phone revealed that he was a ruddy duck.

Jim and I completed our New Year's Day island hike by returning along the tidal inlet to the northern end of the island on the Swamp Trail. Most of the grasses and sedges in the swamp are bleached and semi-prostrate now, with the vivid green of non-native yellow-blooming iris leaves poking up here and there. When we first stepped onto the boardwalk, we saw our boy–girl mallards all lined up and sleeping peacefully *in* the cold shallow water, something that struck us as hilariously improbable from our human perspective.

Walking through the swamp we smelled the citrusy scents of fallen bald-cypress foliage and saw cloud-like drifts of cattail seeds floating on the surface of the low-lying grasses, sedges, and cypress needles. At the northern end of the boardwalk I put my hand under one of these clouds, and the tiny seeds immediately lifted up and set sail on wings of soft white hairs. The extreme lightness and airborne-readiness of these tiny cattail seeds was almost otherworldly. When I closed my eyes, their touch on my hand before lift-off was imperceptible.

We arrived at the northern end of the island in the emerging twilight. Jim is an expert stone-skipper, and while he skipped stones from a mudflat facing Key Bridge, he excitedly called out when he saw the lights come on along K Street *in the water* as reflections. While marveling over the multiple leaps of each of Jim's skipping stones, I sat on a fallen tree and spoke on the phone with Sophie, who was safely back home in Pittsburgh. As we talked, the new moon revealed itself in the skies over Rosslyn, first as chalky and milk-white, and later as a blazing crescent accompanied by a vivid white planet Venus.

Jim and I headed back along the western shore of the island. When we stopped to admire the sycamore tree I named Grandmother, we heard a white-throated sparrow sing "sweetly and plaintively" from a nearby tree. And as we crossed the footbridge to the mainland, a beaver was exploring the Virginia shore in the deepening dusk.

Once back home, we ate more black-eyed peas. After our island adventure, and another meal of lucky peas, I felt ready to face whatever the new year would bring.

January 11th: Winter Beauty Nourishes

This morning Jim is home working on finances, so I ceded my usual workspace on the dining-room table to him and his mound of documents, moved our bicycles from my small office, and brought my laptop to the desk with its view through a sea of evergreen "feral topiary," the oxymoron teenaged Jesse coined a decade ago to describe the rarely pruned woody landscape plants in our yard. Balsam, our "grandkitty," who has been staying here during Sophie's interviews for faculty positions, has just hopped onto the desk. The view over my laptop is now black cat against green backdrop. Birds are chirping in the shrubbery and Balsam the cat is chirping back. She was once a feral cat so no doubt deep memories are stirring within her. Between the bird-like chirps, she lets out longing little cries. My heart goes out to her and her remembrance of the wild, as harsh as it was for her as a young mother cat who lost a litter of kittens on Balsam Mountain in North Carolina before being rescued by some kind and generous women.

While sweeping off the neglected surface of my desk, a small booklet of Thoreau bookmarks fell open to this quote, printed on a painting of a red-winged blackbird singing from a cattail stalk with a willow in the background:

> *May I ever be in as good*
> *spirits as a willow!*
> *How tenacious of life!*
> *How withy! How soon*
> *it gets over its hurts!*
> *They never despair.*[26]

Withy! May I adopt Thoreau's lovely word! Withy, flexible like the willow twig that bends and braids. Withy I will be. How soon I will get over my hurts, and I will never despair.

I will need the black willows of Theodore Roosevelt Island to help me live withily in this era of progressive outgoing "no drama" Obama, who gave his farewell address last evening, and erratic authoritarian Trump, who gives his first press conference in months in less than an hour and whose cabinet picks are now being vetted on the Hill. Every day is a day filled with petty ravaging tweets (the Oscar-winning actress, Meryl Streep, the current object of his revenge tweeting) and new revelations about his business dealings. This morning rumors are swirling that the intelligence community has been in possession of allegations that the Russian government has compromising evidence of Trump's shady business and sexual exploits.

I am trying to learn to cope in this era of uncertainty. I'm spending more time in the woods, on my yoga mat, and with my friends. A week from tomorrow, friends and family from all over the country will begin to arrive here for the Women's March on January 21st, the day after Trump's inauguration. The art of *our* deal is to live fully and joyfully ourselves, while bravely standing up wherever needed. This dance is in the early choreographic stages for me as I teeter between anger and despair, and the desire to effect change while preserving my sanity.

Two days ago I returned to the island to absorb the beauty of a fresh snowfall. Just a dusting, but a dusting is all it takes to transform the landscape. The temperature was in the mid-20s Fahrenheit (around -4C) and the tide was high and still rising when I got out of my car, one of a handful of vehicles in the parking lot. I took a deep breath of cold air as I surveyed the scene. White sycamores lined the island shore across Little River, Grandmother the largest and most magnificent of all. Along the edges of the island and Virginia shoreline, a graceful scalloping of gray-white ice was forming.

Crossing the bridge, I was greeted by the silver maples, basswoods, beeches, and bitternut hickories of the upper canopy, and the pawpaws and spicebush of the lower one. A few small dry nutlike fruits of the basswoods still hung from weathered wheat-colored leafy bracts. All around me the winter leaf litter was dusted with snow that accentuated the outlines of fallen sycamore, beech, and oak leaves, their tannins holding their profiles intact atop the frozen ground. The fallen leaves of the silver maples were gray and crumpled under their gauzy white snow covering, and the basswood and hickory leaves were already breaking down, well on their journey from treetop food production to vital component of the living soil.

I walked to the river's edge to see the thin gray-white ice.

Within the scalloped ice sheets, which reached no more than a few feet out into the largely unfrozen Little River channel, small feathery icy formations sparkled under the thin bright cloud cover. The sun promised to break through as I headed north along the island's western shore, Dave's suggested direction on our last Kingfisher Court walk.

The American hollies along the trail caught my eye against the snow. As I was admiring the hollies, a runner came toward me, dressed all in dark blue, with red running shoes. As I gazed about at other surrounding trees, I remembered the new vocabulary I was sickened to have to learn recently: "woodpecker blonding," describing the discoloration of ash bark once the emerald ash borers have done their murderous work and woodpeckers have followed in their wake, and "ash snap," the way ashes brittly snap in two once robbed of their vascular integrity. I saw many examples of woodpecker blonding and a few of ash snap along the trail. Not so withy, those trees, and I felt compassion for them.

On every island walk, I stop to visit Grandmother with her exposed, whitened, far-reaching roots wrapped around the dark and comforting bedrock of the Sykesville Formation and her commanding Little River view. As I was standing on one of Grandmother's rocks I saw four fairly large ducks in Little River. I recognized them as common mergansers from remembered sightings upriver at Carderock, where I have led budbreak walks during the past few early springs.

The three females were gray with reddish-brown heads, white necks, and reddish bills, and the male was handsomely hued with dark green head, red bill, dark back, and very large white patches on his sides. The male and one female broke away from the larger group and began swimming downstream. The male led and the female followed as they traversed the silver-gray river that was narrowly and evenly rippled by a breeze from the south. The two beautiful ducks were gracefully traveling into the ripples. Just then the sun broke through. In that moment, my whole world came down to these two ducks and the shining liquid-silver river.

I crossed to the eastern shore of the island and climbed out onto the large outcrop north of the swamp near the Shumard oaks, where the alders grow next to an ancient stunted and gnarled American elm. Here, larger ripples were moving over and below the ice sheets surrounding the rock outcrop. As I stood on the rock looking toward Georgetown and the gulls near its shore, I heard musical sounds coming from the river that I had never heard before. One sound was high and tinkling, a little like falling sleet. Then there was a slightly lower sound, not unlike chirping birds (or cats!). Beneath those were the deeper, slower tones of water moving beneath the ice. I also imagined hearing sounds of a crackling fire.

Mesmerized by the symphonic water and ice, I turned around toward the winter-white island just as a large low-flying accipiter, most likely a Cooper's hawk, no more than 10 feet away, slipped silently through the black, bare-branched oaks and down toward the swamp.

I entered the swamp, which felt like a new world with its wintry cloak. The large bitternut hickory near the beginning of the boardwalk was on fire in the lowering golden sunshine. The gray braided bark of the tall straight trunk had taken on a golden glow, and I followed the gold up to the high branches, to the "wiggly twigs" (Kate Maynor's description), with their flame-colored, flame-shaped buds. I always thought of the buds as mustard-toned (either the spicy brown or the classic yellow variety, depending on the light) and half-moon shaped. I had never before seen them as brilliantly lit candles.

The boardwalk was snow-covered and stamped with a few animal and human footprints. As I walked to the heart of the swamp, another runner, a young man, came toward me. Seeing my binoculars, he smiled and happily burst out without breaking stride: "There's a blue jay up ahead!"

I never saw his jay, but I was soon even deeper into a late-afternoon reverie. The swampland was snow-covered, and its watery patches were frozen and brilliantly lit with reflections of the lowering sun. It was very cold, and still, and quiet between planes, and I felt completely happy. My whole being felt nourished by the winter beauty of the swamp, and I experienced instant sympathy and also deep gratitude for those who were across the river in their government offices, wondering what the future would hold.

It felt even colder as I got close to the icy home of the bald-cypress trees along the tidal inlet. I walked out along the side-boardwalk where some of the cypresses live so that I could witness the frozen inlet, a sight I may not see again this year. I could make out the tide still flowing in between the gray-white ice sheets. The black willow twigs were dark and withy against the sky. Nearer the ground, small flocks of gray and white juncos and brown sparrows flitted among the cattail stalks, their dark brown cylindrical fruit clusters spilling pale fluffy seeds from their tops like freshly uncorked champagne.

I passed under the Theodore Roosevelt Bridge and out to the inlet looking south toward Memorial Bridge. A pale nearly full moon shone through the bare trees of Little Island, trees filled with ospreys in summer. As I looked to the south, where the river was trying valiantly to freeze up, I remembered the crash of the Air Florida plane 35 years ago this week that killed one of my colleagues and 73 other people on board. The plane crashed into the 14th Street Bridge, the bridge just south of Memorial Bridge, killing four motorists, before landing in the icy river. A dramatic rescue by a heroic swimmer, and a helicopter rope carrying a female flight attendant, the only crew member to survive the crash, are emblazoned in my memory. For days the plane lay in the frozen river with bodies inside. At the time a friend said the situation called up an arcane word for her: *unshriven*. The passengers lay in their icy tomb, unshriven.

It was a morbid thought for a beautiful afternoon, but this year it's hard to feel immune to catastrophic thought, no matter how joy-filled the afternoon.

I watched part of the president-elect's press conference in between the day's paragraphs, and I feel even more trepidatious imagining what his actions will be during the presidency he will assume in nine days. However, thanks to Jim's daily reading in *The American Patriot's Almanac*, which he shared with me this morning, I know what Theodore Roosevelt did 109 years ago today: He declared the Grand Canyon a national monument. Roosevelt's conservation ethic sprang from a deep abiding love of nature and a prescient knowledge of what could be lost.

I hope our country is withy enough to withstand what we will face in the coming days.

January 18th: A Botanist Visits the Island in the Rain

Rain was pouring down when I met Rod Simmons in the island parking lot yesterday afternoon, but thankfully the temperature was a good deal warmer than on my last visit. Rod is Natural Resource Manager and Plant Ecologist for the City of Alexandria. I had asked him if he would meet me for a walk on the island because he is one of the best botanists I know. I hoped he could answer my long list of questions about island plants and clear up a few botanical mysteries. Rod is a legend, bordering on guru status, for native plant enthusiasts of the Washington region. For several years I served with him on the board of the Maryland Native Plant Society, and he is also active in the Virginia Native Plant Society. Rod's knowledge of plants and plant communities is unsurpassed and, like so many other plant experts I've met over the years here, he is entirely generous with his knowledge.

Rod was smiling broadly as I got out of my car, his curly gray hair not growing any less curly in the rain. I cut my finger in my haste to raise my umbrella after I greeted Rod, so today

I'm perusing sheets of notes that are splattered with blood as well as rain! Thanks to the weather, they are also cursory, to say the least, but no matter. Rod's pronouncements about plants are memorable on their own.

As the rain poured down, I subjected Rod to a deluge of questions before we'd even stepped onto the footbridge to the island. I asked about the hybrid Bartram's oak, a cross between the willow oak and northern red oak, standing sentinel next to the bridge, where it was most likely planted sometime during the twentieth century.

"Does this hybrid occur in nature?" I asked Rod.

"Oh yes," he said.

Later during the walk we would come upon a younger Bartram's oak that seemed to be growing wild near the Theodore Roosevelt Bridge.

Once across the bridge, I steered us northward, into the floodplain forest. Rod pointed out the layers of plant communities as we walked, beginning with silver maple/sycamore closest to the shore to our left, then transitioning to black walnut/boxelder on the slightly higher ground to our right. And beyond and through those trees, we could see the more upland forest of beech, tulip-tree, and red and white oak. Rod was impressed by the first of the bitternut hickories I pointed out to him. He would be even more impressed by the tree near the entrance to the swamp boardwalk on the opposite side of the island, a tree that he suggested we come back and measure for possible champion status.

One of my botanical mysteries involved the island's Shumard oaks, a southern tree on the northern edge of its range here. I knew from *City of Trees* research that the oak is a state rare (S2) species in Maryland and that it grew on Theodore Roosevelt Island. I had identified the two specimens near the Georgetown-facing rock outcrop as probably Shumard, and Sharon Forsyth of the Kingfisher Court and I had guessed that one of the largest trees in the floodplain forest north of the footbridge on the western side of the island was a Shumard.

When I showed Rod the tall, full-crowned tree with its ground-level halo of fallen, reddish-brown, bleached, deeply incised leaves, he nodded in agreement over its identity. This gave me a happy chill. Such a magnificent tree and a Shumard! The leaves are very much like the deeply lobed leaves of the scarlet oak, DC's official tree, but the acorn cap is shallow, like a northern red oak's acorn (which resembles a French beret). And you wouldn't find a scarlet oak growing naturally in the floodplain.

Rod loved the floodplain forest. He told me it had been a while since he'd visited the island. There is so much to occupy him in his hometown parks. I always knew he was a good botanist. What I couldn't have predicted was how much joy he'd express as he explored the shoreline trails that have become so dear to me. As we marveled over Grandmother Sycamore and her precarious perch on riverside bedrock, Rod came upon a trove of bleached winter grasses, and I struggled to make furious rain-spattered notes. There were three species of rye grasses along the trail near Grandmother: riverbank wild rye (*Elymus riparius*), "tall and drooping"; Virginia wild rye (*Elymus virginicus*), "thick and bracted"; and hairy wild rye (*Elymus villosus*), "delicate, hairy, and drooping," but the hairs only visible with a hand lens. Rod also brought my attention to a tall sweet wood reed or Indian grass plant (*Cinna arundinacea*) near the rye. Surrounding the rye grasses and the wood reed were the ubiquitous wild oats of Theodore Roosevelt Island. All grasses were bleached a lovely reddish wheat color, a color enhanced by the rain. And to further round out the graminoid picture, Rod said we should look for the wild rice I thought I'd seen in the fall.

Rounding the northern edge of the island and heading east, Rod spotted a humongous trumpet creeper vine that he also mentioned could be of record size. He cleared up another mystery when he told me that the reddish-berried shrub to the right of the trail heading toward the Georgetown-facing side of the island was coralberry, a plant whose native range he said was sketchy due to its widespread naturalization. We both noted that a crew had been busy trying to beat back the invasive bush honeysuckle that is an island scourge. I've got to get in touch with Friends of Theodore Roosevelt Island to find out about invasives removal programs and how they are staffed and funded, if funded at all. And in the Trump era, what will happen to an already pitiful shoestring budget to deal with invasive plants in the national parks system?

We sadly shook our heads as we walked through acres of dead and dying ash trees with their telltale "woodpecker blonding." We could hear woodpeckers happily hammering all around us, finding food and communicating with one another.

Rod expanded my graminoid knowledge even further as he pointed out the evergreen leaves of various sedges of the *Carex* genus. James's sedge (*Carex jamesii*) in the northern floodplain forest, blunt broom sedge (*Carex tribuloides*) and Emory's sedge (*Carex emoryi*) in the tidal marsh. I also have a mention of eastern woodland sedge (*Carex blanda*) in my rain-spattered notes.

Walking past the Georgetown-facing outcrop (hereafter referred to as Georgetown Rock!) and the possibly record-busting bitternut hickory, we stepped onto the boardwalk and entered the northern end of the swamp with its old silver maples and boxelders. The maples bore plump reddish flower buds, and the green twigs of the female boxelders still held onto a few paired samaras. The ephemeral winter wonderland had dissolved in the rain.

We walked out onto the bald-cypress turnout and talked about how the area had hosted a cypress swamp prior to the Ice Age. Rod agreed that the planted trees here looked right at home with their earth-level haloes of knees. He also exclaimed over the height of the ironweed, surmising that it might be tall ironweed (*Vernonia gigantea*) rather than New York ironweed (*Vernonia noveboracensis*).

I asked Rod about the two species of cattail I thought I'd identified: common cattail (*Typha latifolia*), the most common species in the Piedmont, and narrow-leaved cattail (*Typha angustifolia*), more often found on the Coastal Plain. As we stood on the very edges of the Piedmont and Coastal Plain, Rod verified the two species and also mentioned that a hybrid between the two of them (*Typha x glauca*) was also likely.

Back on the main part of the boardwalk, I showed Rod my favorite frame for the Kennedy Center, a border of black willow and common cattail in the swampy foreground. Rod loved it and said he could *smell* aspirin on the air. The willow is the source of salicylic acid, a potent medicine known to Indian tribes and the main ingredient in aspirin. As much as I tried to smell aspirin on the moist air myself, my olfactory detectors fell short.

We walked under the Theodore Roosevelt Bridge and out to the inlet between the main island and Little Island. Rod was taken with the beauty of the scene, looking out across the wide Potomac to the Memorial Bridge and adjacent Virginia shoreline. We didn't see the wild rice, but I showed him my biggest botanical mystery: the hybrid oak that Sharon and I have puzzled over. We found the crazy leaves that are somewhere between chinquapin oak and white oak lying liberally upon the ground, but in the winter rain we couldn't find the tree. Rod thought our guess that it might be Deam's oak (*Quercus x deamii*), a cross between the chinquapin and the white, was a possibility, but we're going to have to get more information about the oak later in the year. And first, we're going to have to find the tree!

As we headed toward the Upland Trail, Rod enthusiastically noted the size and stature of two additional bottomland trees: the large American elm near the restrooms, and my *feng shui* silver maple next to the Theodore Roosevelt Island Bridge. In the uplands, he was really taken with the black walnuts near the Mason home site and agreed that they were impressively old and could easily date to John Mason's time. He was not as enamored of the upland woods, which, unlike the floodplain forest, seemed to be more the result of human hands than natural occurrence. Many of the trees in the uplands were planted by a CCC crew under the direction of Frederick Law Olmsted Jr. during the 1930s, and that might explain why eastern hemlocks and even Kentucky coffee trees grow among the oaks, hickories, and tulip-trees.

Before leaving the island, Rod expressed the desire to come back with other botanists and natural resource people to explore later in the year. Needless to say, that was music to my island-loving ears.

January 29th: A Wild Inauguration Day Walk

The pain and trauma of Inauguration Day was softened by a wild walk in Rock Creek Park, and the arrival of friends and family from all over the country to participate in the Women's March the following day. Jamie Raskin, our newly elected Congressman from Maryland's Eighth District, asked me to lead a nature walk for him in Rock Creek Park on inauguration afternoon, along with the first 75 people to register. Most of our out-of-town group of marchers joined us for the 4 p.m. walk, four hours after the swearing in on Capitol Hill.

Jamie was one of at least 67 members of Congress who chose not to attend the inauguration, many of them citing a Trump slight to Congressman John Lewis, the Civil Rights leader who was the target of one of his tweets. Trump called Lewis all talk and no action after Lewis questioned Trump's legitimacy. Lewis still bears the scars from a skull fracture at the hands of Alabama State Troopers during the 1965 Civil Rights march across Selma's Edmund Pettus Bridge that became known as "Bloody Sunday." I know that Jamie agonized over the decision not to attend his first inauguration as a newly elected Member of Congress. He did so in solidarity with Lewis.

The afternoon was overcast and gloomy and it had rained a little earlier in the day. It perfectly suited the mood of the 75-plus people who gathered on Boundary Bridge for our nature walk. After Jamie introduced me, with praise for my Rock Creek Park book, I immediately focused on the task at hand: doling out some heaping helpings of nature therapy to the shell-shocked group assembled on the bridge. I applauded Jamie for his strong environmental record as a Maryland state senator, noting that as a constitutional law professor he—unlike our newly inaugurated president—is acquainted with the Constitution, and added that he was sending *30* buses to the Women's March from Silver Spring the following day. Then I turned my attention to the place where we were gathered.

"If you peek over the side of Boundary Bridge, you'll see that the date 1935 is carved into the concrete," I said. "This 82-year-old bridge crossing Rock Creek at the Maryland/DC line was a New Deal project of the Franklin Delano Roosevelt administration."

"Once we step off the bridge and into the floodplain forest," I added, "we'll be entering the nation's capital and the oldest urban national park in the country, created in 1890 by an Act of Congress, the same year Yosemite became a national park."

After giving this little bit of restorative history to help ground us in the face of shaky current affairs, I asked everyone to look up into the trees surrounding the bridge: the magnificent American elm with its "rickrack" twigs and buds, the chalky-white American sycamores (sisters of Grandmother), the tall straight tulip-tree with its candelabras of clustered samaras, and the cinnamon-barked river birch leaning far out over Rock Creek and bearing preformed catkins on its delicate twigs.

I knew there wouldn't be much more botanizing on the walk. Even as we set out, dusk was descending, and I felt that what we all needed was to walk as long and far as possible, breathing in the healthy air of the urban forest. I stopped once during the walk to point out an iconic Rock Creek Park winter sight: the smooth gray bark, wheat-colored "marcescent" leaves, and elegant pointed buds of the American beech.

"You notice these trees in winter even from your car windows on Beach Drive," I said.

When we had climbed to the upland woods, I asked my friend Terrie Daniels to read a Wendell Berry poem that seemed perfect for the occasion. As we all grew silent, overlooking Rock Creek under the canopy of native oaks, Terrie read, with quiet passion, Berry's powerful poem about the respite from cares offered by nature: "The Peace of Wild Things."

After a short yet reverential stop at a massive and ancient northern red oak, and a few more minutes of hiking, we climbed out onto the rock outcrop that I dubbed the "Laurel Ledge" ten winters ago. There, Jamie held "woodland court," answering questions about what he planned to do in Congress. He was forthright with us about the difficulty of the tasks ahead, but he sounded strong and resolute about his progressive agenda.

January 30th: The Women's March

The reason I am not stark raving mad at this moment in time, apart from my relationship with nature, is the Women's March held in DC the day after the inauguration, and the sister marches that were simultaneously held around the world. The millions of participants in these marches were part of a global movement created in order to share our values and uplift each other in the face of despair.

That one sweeping gesture has become my metaphorical Sykesville Formation—the half-billion to billion-year-old rock formation underlying Theodore Roosevelt Island—in this era of shifting and shaking ground. We created something palpable, if temporary; meaningful in the ways that I find walking in nature meaningful.

While sitting by the fire in our living room on inauguration night, I suggested to family and friends who were gathered for the Women's March that we focus our intentions for the march the next day. We jotted our fears on individual scraps of paper and took turns tossing them into the fire. We then shared our hopes for the following day, before heading to our beds, couches, and floors to get some sleep before the big day.

The speeches weren't due to start until 10 a.m., and when we arrived at 8:30 Independence Avenue was already packed and we weren't able to get anywhere near the main stage. Everyone was in an ebullient mood, and good energy freely flowed. Pointedly hilarious signs and hand-knitted pink "pussy hats" with cats' ears were sprinkled throughout the packed crowd. My favorite signs: "If I make my uterus a corporation, will you stop regulating it?" and "Girls just want to have FUN-damental rights!"

I was happy to note how many men there were in the crowd, including a tall man in front of me who was blocking my view. I turned to Terrie and whispered in all good humor: "Isn't it just like a man to block your view with his pussy hat?"

The opening song by Jennifer Elizabeth Kreisberg, who sang in her ancient Native American language, was one of the most powerful things I have ever heard. It sounded like a wail from the Earth itself. We were in sight of the Museum of the American Indian, and I had flashbacks to another march, near the autumnal equinox of 2004, when thousands of native peoples processed along the National Mall to honor the opening of the museum.

Among the eloquent speakers at the Women's March, Gloria Steinem was the standout for me, still youthfully strong in her eighties as she spoke about women's rights and social justice.

"Make sure you introduce yourselves to each other and decide what we're going to do tomorrow, and tomorrow and tomorrow," she urged. "We're never turning back!"

I also loved hearing from the new senator from California, Kamala Harris.

"We are at an inflection point in the history of our country," she said in a strong, clear voice. "I think of this as being a moment in time similar to that moment in time when my parents met when they were active in the Civil Rights Movement at the University of California Berkeley in the 1960s." She went on: "We must re-commit our power and our purpose and let's make today a beginning. Let's buckle in because it's going to be a bumpy ride."

Terrie and I wildly high-fived each other as Harris eloquently spoke, sharing ridiculously premature yet exuberant hopes for 2020.

Standing in a closely packed crowd for five hours grows wearying even in the most inspired circumstances, and crowd chants emerged and grew urgent: "Let us march, let us march!" We grew frustrated when the organizers seemed not to be hearing us. Unbeknown to us, *there was nowhere to march.*

From our limited perspective, and with cell service and email shut down due to overwhelming volume, we had no way of knowing that Independence Avenue was wall-to-wall people for the entirety of the march route, and the National Mall was filled with many times more people than had gathered for the inauguration the previous day. When I ran into a friend the following day in Rock Creek Park, she opined, "It wasn't a march; it was an occupation."

For me, the empowering numbers and the spirit of the people who gathered in Washington and around the world that day gave me hope and faith to carry on. I was heartened to learn that marches were held on every continent, including Antarctica. I was especially touched to read about a patient who marched up and down his hospital corridor with his IV pole.

The next morning our group of march participants sat by another blazing fire in our living room, sharing our immediate and long-term goals before fanning out around the country. Doctors and psychologists among us said they would work with refugees and Planned Parenthood, and two young women expressed a desire to run for elected office. Dr. Cathy Cornell and her friends would deliver a petition to Senator Susan Collins of Maine, signed by 75 scientists of their state, opposing the Pruitt nomination for director of the EPA.

The women's marches were a critical show of international unity that I suspect will resonate for months and years to come. For me personally, the warmth of the gathering of friends and family, and the good humor we shared along the march route and around the fire, was a balm for my troubled mind and aching heart. And I imagine this was true for many of my neighbors whose floors were also lined with sleeping bags.

Chapter Eight

February—Grandmother Sycamore on Little River

February 7th: The End of Longing?

I begin this entry with a primal scream. Last year was Earth's hottest year on record. The second hottest year was 2015, and 2014 was third. Here in Washington, we've barely had winter weather, and only the most negligible snowfalls. Today it's headed into the high 60s Fahrenheit (about 20C). Meanwhile, we have just inaugurated a president who wants to gut the EPA, drill for oil and gas in national parks, and revive the dirtiest fossil fuel of all: coal. When you live in a gilded cage high above Fifth Avenue, who cares for the lowly lives of frogs and butterflies or an antiquated notion called "biological diversity"? Since my last entry, I've walked on Theodore Roosevelt Island with the conservation biologist who coined that term.

I am learning that living in the era of Trump requires complicated mental choreography. We have to learn how to shield ourselves from the constant barrage of upsetting headlines about everything from disastrous cabinet picks; a travel ban on seven Muslim countries (currently blocked at least until later today by court order); petulant, juvenile early-morning tweets duly reported upon by the press; and the constant egregious defiance of peace and civility, while simultaneously staying tuned in enough to take action where needed. Which Is Everywhere.

Ten years ago this winter I began my book, *A Year in Rock Creek Park*, with a more subdued primal scream after witnessing spring beauties abnormally in bud on New Year's Day during another too-warm winter. There is something so innocent about the opening pages of that book. They are filled with longing. *Longing for snow. Longing for a coherent global response to the unfolding nightmare of climate change. Longing* is something stronger than hope. It's tensile, and it's done with the whole heart. I look back on the younger middle-aged woman who wrote those pages, and I have to confess to her that today I'm beyond longing for snow. I'm deep into a late middle-aged grudging acceptance of the too-warm winter that is part of the bigger, much scarier, picture. It's not that I'm close to giving up the fight. I'm filled with fight. But the fight itself has robbed me of some of the sweetness that makes longing possible.

During these dark times, Theodore Roosevelt Island has become my literal and figurative bedrock. In some sort of convoluted way, it's kept some longing alive, because it's so hard to get to. I can't visit daily, sometimes not even weekly, but when I drink my first glass of ice-cold water straight from the tap in the morning, I think of the mallards, mergansers, and ruddy ducks paddling around in the cold river it comes from, and I *long* for the sight of a kingfisher diving for a fish. I picture Grandmother Sycamore surveying the Little River scene cloaked in her glorious white inner bark as my day begins. I wonder if the tide is high or low, ebbing or flowing. Perhaps I haven't reached the end of longing.

February 13th: Connections

On my way to the Blue Ridge Mountains for a winter getaway with Jim three days ago, I planned my route to include a stop at Theodore Roosevelt Island. As I walked across the footbridge at low tide on a cold, bright afternoon, a great blue heron was standing still as a statue in the mudflats along the Virginia shore, the breeze ruffling his or her slate-gray neck feathers. A single gull was poking about in the mud nearby, and a lone kayaker dressed in a deep blue jacket and black pants quietly paddled his sleek white craft under the bridge. The river was green under a partially overcast sky, and the tide about as low as it can go at full moon, a moon due to be partially eclipsed that evening, with its view blocked in DC and northern Virginia by thickening cloud cover.

All along the western island shore, the sycamores lifted their ghostly limbs to the afternoon, their twigs ornamented with round balls of tightly packed single-seeded fruits, which were bouncing merrily on the breeze. As always, Grandmother Sycamore reigned supreme, leaning out over Little River, her roots wrapped around bedrock and into island and river-bottom soil. Thin layers of ice coated parts of the island mudflats, testament to the real wintriness of the afternoon, while above the ice-flecked mud, silver maples reached their round red flower buds to the sky. Some had already opened to reveal golden stamens, harbingers of spring.

Now, as I look up to the Blue Ridge and the high pastures of Sky Meadows State Park through the arching windows of a room at the Ashby Inn in Paris, Virginia on a very windy cold morning, I think about the importance of connections. I wanted to connect with the island before heading deeper into the Piedmont and then the mountains. Last evening Jim and I drove along the south fork of the Shenandoah River at dusk, the water reflecting the gold and pink of the setting sun and the bone-white sycamores lining the shores. Just north of here, the Shenandoah flows into the Potomac, and the Potomac flows down to Theodore Roosevelt Island. So here in the mountains I feel connected to the beloved island in the familiar river. I'm almost caught up in my backlogged chronology of island visits and other events.

Six days after the Women's March, my naturalist friend Wendy Paulson came to town, and she and I invited a small band of birders and conservationists to join us for an island walk. As this group came together, it included world-famous conservation biologist Tom Lovejoy (Betsy's dad), who coined the very term "biological diversity," internationally prominent tropical biologist and author Adrian Forsyth (Sharon's husband), and several others who are renowned in their fields. The reach and breadth of love for the natural world, and for Theodore Roosevelt Island, always uplifts me. I could only chuckle inside, imagining myself leading a nature walk for this distinguished crew.

When Wendy lived in Washington during the time when her husband, Hank Paulson, served as Secretary of the Treasury, we did many walks together, where she led on birding and I often filled in with plant lore. As I picked her up downtown where she was staying, she handed me a folder containing several sheets of paper and told me they were excerpts from her DC nature journals, including passages describing walks that she had led on Theodore Roosevelt Island.

Wendy and I drove to the island on a properly cold and wintry day and met the group in the parking lot, where we stood in a circle under the Bartram's oak and introduced ourselves. When it was Wendy's turn, she told the story of how I had "talked over" a Connecticut warbler sighting on one of her walks, with my exuberance for some plant. She has told this story before and I guess I will never live it down. As a consequence, I always say to people at the outset of my walks, "If I'm nattering on about some plant and you see or hear an interesting bird, *please* interrupt me, because the plants aren't going anywhere!"

We saw few birds on our wintry walk, but Wendy pointed out that getting out of the single digits for species in January is a good thing. At least we managed that. After examining the silver maple flower buds just over the bridge, a handful opening to reveal their stamens, we headed north into the floodplain forest. I showed them the large Shumard oak to the right of the trail, and Sharon was especially happy to have had our diagnostic suspicions confirmed by Rod Simmons. We looked closely at the fuzzy round reddish flower buds of one of the pawpaws, along with the naked leaf bud at the tip of the twig that has been called "Audubon's paintbrush" in reference to a rumor that the great nature painter John James Audubon once painted with one.

The group moseyed along, visiting with each other, occasionally stopping for sightings of Carolina chickadees, tufted titmice, and various woodpeckers in the forest along the shoreline. Alison Greenberg, Executive Director of Georgetown Heritage, took some wonderful photos of downy woodpeckers, which she shared with us via email after the walk. Sharon carried her telescope mounted on a tripod, at the ready should we see any ducks or grebes out on the water. I pointed out a few plants along the route, including the bitternut hickory at the top of the swamp boardwalk, which drew appreciative "oohs" and "ahs." As we walked I enjoyed talking with Nick Lapham about his organic farm in the Blue Ridge Mountains (not far from where we're staying now).

A bald eagle flew overhead as we wandered down the boardwalk through the swamp. When we reached the bald-cypresses, Sharon said that she still had her cone from our first Kingfisher Court walk last fall, and she said she takes it out to smell first thing in the morning and whenever she's feeling down. Wendy said she had never smelled a cypress cone, so I scouted around until I found a really fragrant fragment of one that I could hand to her.

We walked under the Theodore Roosevelt Bridge and out to the inlet between Theodore Roosevelt Island and Little Island. From there we saw hundreds of Canada geese on the river and a pair of great blue herons engaged in a fascinating if gawky dance. I was standing with Wendy and Tom Lovejoy as we watched the herons, and Wendy sighed and said, "We've just got to get people out to see this."

If our leaders could see the world through the eyes of Wendy or Tom or any of the people on the island with us that day, they would see a world of wonder in desperate need of our loving protection. In Rachel Carson's words: "Wonder and humility are wholesome emotions, and they do not exist side by side with a lust for destruction."[27]

A few days later Sharon led a long-promised expedition expressly to find ducks along local stretches of the Potomac from Fletcher's Cove to Alexandria. We watched ducks on the river in DC and at Constitution Gardens on the National Mall and then headed over to Tide Lock Park in Alexandria.

From the shores of Tide Lock, looking out over the wide tidal Potomac, I saw more ducks in one place than I had ever seen in my life, and I got good looks at all of them thanks to the magic of Sharon's scope. We saw greater and lesser scaup (Sharon estimated the number of the latter to approach 1,000), about 200 redheads, 20 canvasbacks, a few buffleheads, more ruddy ducks, black ducks, mallards, coots, and as a real bonus, common loons, horned grebes, and pied-billed grebes.

People often tell me, after attending one of my walks or reading one of my books, that they are stunned by the diversity of plants in and around our city. Now I know how they feel. How could there be so many species of ducks paddling in and around DC, in such numbers—and of which I've been entirely ignorant?

It grew cold out along the water, and after closely examining each species through the scope, I gave Sharon a shivery goodbye and drove down the George Washington Memorial Parkway to Mount Vernon, car heat cranked high. I remembered how, as a young woman, I had experienced the joy of discovering George Washington's love of trees, and the awe I felt when I first stood under trees he had planted, trees which are still growing at Mount Vernon but were inaccessible to me on this winter afternoon 40 years later because the gates had already closed for the day. I was still shivering a little as I headed northward on the parkway, but my heart was warmed by the beauty of the widening Potomac south of the city and the legacy of our tree-loving founding president.

February 23rd: More Island Visits and "Halcyon Days"

It was heartening for me to read over my recent writings just now to remind myself that, despite near snowlessness in the DC area this winter, we have had a bit of cold here in recent days. The thermometer stands at 70 degrees (21C) as I write at 11:15 a.m., and it's supposed to go up to 75F/24C this afternoon [footnote: Dulles Airport near Washington broke a record at 77F/25C this day] with a high of 73 (23C) tomorrow. There is no snow in sight, and March 1st is less than a week away. This snow-loving climate worrier hasn't given up on the winter of 2017, but she is all too aware that its days are seriously numbered.

During our too-warm winters, I'm haunted by the phrase "Halcyon Days." In Greek mythology, Halcyon was married to King Ceyx. She was distraught when he drowned at sea, and so the gods took pity on her and turned both Ceyx and Halcyon into kingfishers. *Halcyon* is the genus name of some of the Old World kingfishers, and our belted kingfisher's binomial name is *Megaceryle alcyon* ("alcyon" is Greek for Halcyon). When Zeus decreed that Halcyon would lay her eggs near the shore in winter, her eggs kept getting washed away by stormy seas. So at the advice of the other gods, he decided to give her a period of balmy weather during winter for nesting, and these became known as the Halcyon Days. Halcyon Days are days of peace and calm, a reprieve from actual and metaphorical winter.

How could Halcyon Days ever be a bad thing? And yet, are they not bad here in Washington, as our spells of too-warm winter weather presage more warming to come?

Soon after I wrote about my impromptu drive to Mount Vernon, I read an Adrian Higgins column in the *Washington Post* titled: "George Washington Would Recognize Today's Mount Vernon Garden, but Not the Weather." According to Adrian, longtime garden columnist for the *Post*, Mount Vernon gardeners have had to drastically modify their pruning schedules and processes for fruit trees now that winters are so mild. This morning I exchanged emails with my friend Anne Sturm, who lives in Montgomery County's Agricultural Reserve near Sugarloaf Mountain. We shared our concerns for our friend Gene Kingsbury who owns and manages a peach and apple orchard near the mountain that has been in his family for more than a hundred years. Last winter Gene suffered huge losses after a spring freeze. When the trees respond to winter warmth and break bud too early, they are vulnerable to late-season freezes.

The spring peepers and wood frogs have already begun their breeding choruses, about two weeks ahead of normal. I'm worried about them because the vernal pools where they lay their eggs hold so little water after this dry winter. This season's tadpole brood probably won't have time to mature before what little water there is evaporates. The vernal pools near Boundary Bridge in Rock Creek Park are bone dry, so there will probably be no mating of wood frogs, spring peepers, or spotted salamanders there this year. In past years I've watched those pools dry up too early; I have never seen them hold no water at all. Perhaps we'll have some appreciable rains before the equinox.

On the national stage, Scott Pruitt, with his allegiance to the fossil fuel industry and his disdain for environmental regulations, is now installed at the EPA. Only one Republican senator voted against his confirmation, and that was the one to whom my friend from Maine, Dr. Cathy Cornell, hand-delivered the petition signed by 75 scientists in opposition: Susan Collins of Cathy's home state. Immigrants are terrified by the draconian new roundups and deportation policies, transgender students lost their bathroom-choice rights with a stroke of Trump's pen this week, and, on every front, policies in direct opposition to what I believe to be in the best interests of humanity and the planet are championed by our new president and Republican congress. Meanwhile Trump's ties to Russian actors, who are believed to have attempted to tip the election in his favor, may never be fully and adequately investigated, and Congress just got rid of the cyber-security board overseeing the voting process.

Almost every time I delve into contemporary affairs on the national front, I despair. I receive daily reminders from various progressive groups to lobby my Congress members about a whole range of issues, but, living in a largely blue (Democratic) state, there's only so much impact I can have.

That is one of the reasons why my visits to the island, where the natural world carries on, have taken on such monumental importance to my sense of well-being.

Late Saturday afternoon, I biked to the island via the Capital Crescent Trail from Bethesda to the Potomac, where I saw a pair of common mergansers paddling, splashing, and diving near the group of little rocky islands known as the Three Sisters. I carried my bike up a flight of steps to the towpath and then pedaled along the golden path, over a small footbridge spanning the canal, and on over to Key Bridge. The afternoon was unseasonably warm, and throngs of bikers and walkers were taking advantage of the halcyon weather, crossing the bridge between Georgetown and Rosslyn.

I stopped to take in the view of Theodore Roosevelt Island from the height of the bridge. The wide silver-blue Potomac River stretched out below, flowing between the capital city and the Virginia shoreline. In the midst of the river in the near distance, the wooded island with its curvy, tree-lined, intermittently rocky shores divided the Potomac into the Georgetown Channel to the east and Little River to the west. All along the northern shore of the island, the sunlit trunks and limbs of sycamores added a dazzling creamy-gold accent to the brown and gray deciduous trees reaching from shoreline to island interior. And on the island's western shores, most magnificent of all: Grandmother Sycamore, leaning out over the Little River channel, her white bark drenched in late-afternoon sun.

Pedaling down the ramp to the Mount Vernon Trail, I saw more stunning views of Grandmother and her island. I texted pictures from the bridge and the ramp to family members and to Tweed Roosevelt, the great-grandson of TR with whom I'd been in recent communication regarding an upcoming documentary about the island. Tweed is President of the Theodore Roosevelt Association, the organization that donated the island to the US government as a presidential memorial in the 1930s. By the time I reached the island I had heard back from everyone—my family exclaiming over the beauty of the scene, and Tweed wanting to talk.

I crossed the footbridge to the island and called Tweed. We talked about his upcoming trip to Washington with his son, Winthrop, and I offered to lead a nature walk for them during their Washington visit. I walked back over the bridge, got off the call, and pedaled my bike back to DC on the Theodore Roosevelt Bridge. From the bridge I was able to look directly down on the swamp boardwalk to see the last of the island's visitors winding their way through the cattails and bald-cypresses in the deepening twilight. I rode past the Watergate, where early cherries were in bloom, and then back along the Rock Creek trail to the Mall.

Heading up 15th Street, northwest to Jim's office (where I

would pop my bike in the back of his truck for the lazy woman's uphill return to Chevy Chase), I came upon a musician singing John Lennon's "Imagine" on a street corner near the Treasury Department and in sight of the White House. As I dropped a donation in his bucket, I asked him: "Will you keep playing this song for the next four years?"

By the time I had reached Jim's office, Tweed had sent an email to several Roosevelt family members, Congressman French Hill of Arkansas (a supporter of national parks and a fan of TR), the board chair of Friends of Theodore Roosevelt Island, and several others, inviting them to a walk I would be leading on Wednesday.

The next day, Sunday, I returned to the island in the afternoon. The parking lot was so jammed I had to wait for 20 minutes to get a spot. Solitude is easy to come by in Washington's parks during the week. I love the weekday quiet, and I enjoy the weekend crowds almost as much, despite the occasional inconvenience of waiting for a parking spot. On any DC woodland trail you will hear many languages spoken by people of all ages on a Saturday, Sunday, or holiday.

I crossed the bridge and began preparing for my walk for Tweed, making notes on my smartphone about the woody plants along the route. It was daunting to prepare to lead an island walk for direct descendants of the man it memorializes and for the president of the association that granted the island to the United States. However, I was soon soothed by the comforting familiarity of the scene. The fuzzy little gold and red flowers of the silver maple trees greeted me in great profusion, many more open than on the previous day. The tide was high as I walked north along the riverside, looking for fuzzy red pawpaw and tiny round green spicebush flower buds to show to the Roosevelt group. When I arrived at the boardwalk, I heard one little piping call from a single spring peeper, sweet amphibian chorister of earliest spring. High in a silver maple a fat gray squirrel was making fast, frenetic work of a twig surely flavorful with flowing sap. The cattails lining the tidal inlet were all in party mode, their "corks" overflowing with cascades of champagne-frothing seeds.

When I reached the southern end of the boardwalk, I stayed north of the Roosevelt Bridge so that I could check out two arboreal grand dames on its northern side: the *feng shui* silver maple and an ancient American elm near the restrooms. Both were in full bloom, their crowns adorned with tiny fuzzy flowers. Against the dusky sky, the elm looked like a tree in an aged daguerreotype.

I decided to return via the eastern stretch of the Upland Trail with its iconic city-views through leafless trees. Three deer crossed my path as I moseyed through the oak and beech forest toward the hemlocks and tulip-trees. Just then a full sweet chorus of spring peepers rose from the maple swamp below.

I sat myself down at the base of a hickory tree in order to fully savor the sound. Spring peepers, which are tiny, rarely seen chorus frogs, have been described as sounding like sleigh bells. I can't imagine a sweeter sound than a full chorus on the first evening of budding spring. The sound is a blend of woodland joy, seasonal hope, and sweet lust! Hearing it you can't help but smile. I sat under the hickory tree grinning in the gathering twilight, a spring-like chill emanating from the earth after the warmth of the afternoon, my reverie broken only by the occasional streaking aircraft overhead. When it got seriously dark, I pulled myself up and tore myself away from my woodland perch, a bright Venus lighting my way back over the footbridge to the Virginia shore.

Chapter Nine

March — Phenology Anxiety

March 3rd: Visiting the Island with the Roosevelts

Three days later I was back in the TRI parking lot, meeting Tweed, his cousin, Dr. Susan Roosevelt Weld (also a great-grandchild of TR), and great-great-grandson, Tweed's son Winthrop. Joanna Sturm, who had made email introductions between Tweed and me, was out of town and unable to join us. Nicole Goldstein, trustee of the Theodore Roosevelt Association and board member of Friends of Theodore Roosevelt Island (FoTRI), fellow board members Sam Sharp and Dr. John Doolittle, and several FoTRI volunteers, as well as a representative from Congressman French Hill's staff, also joined us for our walk.

Once our group was assembled and I had rather awkwardly dispensed stick-on name tags, something I do on every walk I lead, we started across the bridge. Winthrop, a delightful young man, is a birder like his great-great-grandfather. He was especially delighted to see the wood ducks and common mergansers we spotted while looking south over Little River from the footbridge. The tide was just shy of its lowest point.

As we stood on the bridge, I tried to communicate my love for the island attributes that I find so compelling: its Piedmont-meets-Coastal-Plain terrain at the fall line; the beauty of the shoreline through the seasons in ebbing and flowing tides; the tall trees of the floodplain forest and the upland woods; the plants of the swamp; the bird life; and the life of the city all around, in the water, on the bridges, and in the skies. They all smiled, somewhat skeptically, as I tried to sell the planes as part of the scene. Tweed expressed his concern about their effect on the birds.

We crossed the bridge to the edge of the island, where Roosevelt family members and friends were delighted with the silver maple blooms and the wheat-colored marcescent leaves of the beech trees in the woods beyond. I had decided to front-load the walk with a bit of botany, and I urged everyone to "scratch and sniff" a fragrant spicebush twig and to look closely at the fuzzy round reddish flower buds and the terminal leaf bud of the pawpaw, often called "Audubon's paintbrush." When we reached the tall Shumard oak, verified recently by Rod, everyone was impressed by the height of the magnificent tree and the breadth of its crown. Sam said that when you look at a map showing 3D satellite-imagery of the island in the summer, the crown of this tree completely obscures the trail.

From the Shumard we wandered over to the shoreline, where I showed them the newly swelling catkins of the musclewood, and pointed out a tall cottonwood. It's of the same species that grows along the Little Missouri River in the Dakota badlands, where a young Roosevelt hunted and cattle-ranched, healing his broken heart after his mother and his wife died on the same day. His Elkhorn ranch house was built from cottonwood.

In one of his most poetic passages, TR wrote of the view from his porch and the trees surrounding his Dakota home:

In the hot noontide hours of midsummer the broad ranch veranda, always in the shade, is almost the only spot where a man can be comfortable; but here he can sit for hours at a time, leaning back in his rocking chair, as he reads or smokes, or with half-closed, dreamy eyes gazes across the shallow, nearly dry river-bed to the wooded bottoms opposite, and to the plateaus lying back of them. Against the sheer white faces of the cliffs, that come down without a break, the dark green tree-tops stand out in bold relief. In the hot, lifeless air all objects that are not near by seem to sway and waver. There are few sounds to break the stillness. From the upper branches of the cottonwood trees overhead, whose shimmering, tremulous leaves are hardly ever quiet, but if the wind stirs at all, rustle and quiver and sigh all day long, comes every now and then the soft, melancholy cooing of the mourning dove, whose voice always seems far away and expresses more than any other sound in nature the sadness of gentle, hopeless, never-ending grief.[28]

Once again, I'm struck by the eloquence of Roosevelt's evocative nature writing.

As we were admiring the cottonwood's island neighbor, Grandmother Sycamore, and her far-reaching roots, I noticed some fresh beaver activity at the base of another nearby tree. As soon as we saw the telltale shavings at the base of the tree that looked as freshly gnawed as the night before, Winthrop began searching the mudflat in front of us for tracks, and everyone else followed suit. I snapped a photo that shows two of Roosevelt's great-grandchildren and a great-great-grandson examining the mud for tracks, just as their naturalist ancestor would have done.

By now we were all engaged in a free-ranging conversation about Theodore Roosevelt Island and its future. As President of the Theodore Roosevelt Association, Tweed is actively engaged in discussing plans to more fully express TR's legacy as president and conservationist on the island. Tweed has a vision of creating several interactive stations around the island that educate people about various aspects of his great-grandfather's presidency. [2020 note: Recently, the Theodore Roosevelt Association, the National Park Service, and Friends of Theodore Roosevelt Island collaborated to create and place several interactive wayside signs highlighting the history of the island and TR's legacy as a lifelong naturalist and conservationist.]

We discussed whether TR had ever visited the island as president. Tweed said he had always thought not, but that he's been mulling over a passage in French Ambassador Jean Jules Jusserand's autobiography, *What Me Befell*, that indicates a visit to a Potomac island near the White House that sounds like what is now known as Theodore Roosevelt Island. Jusserand was a frequent companion on the president's ambitious outings in Rock Creek Park and along the Potomac River in all weathers. A memorial bench in Rock Creek Park honors the ambassador.

Ambassador Jusserand's passage to which Tweed referred reveals the intrepid side of the multidimensional TR, more familiar to most of us than the poetic writer of prose about cottonwoods, mourning doves, and his beloved rocking chair. The ambassador wrote:

We were sometimes led to the Potomac islands, now beautiful gardens, full of flowers, but then mud shoals, with thick cane-brakes so high that we had to follow in close formation not to lose track of our leader, and with unexpected watery holes into which one stumbled knee-deep, by which I really mean up to the knees. We knew that to frown at anything was mere folly, we would be asked to take the obstacle all the same and be viewed with scorn as a punishment. We were once led at dusk, by a drenching rain, to the Potomac. How the President could, so near the White House, discover such muddy ways was a mystery, but he did; we had not walked ten minutes before we were splashing each other with a mud of rarest blackness. Along the bank we came upon a dredge from which emerged an iron drain-pipe reaching a near-by island. The president suggested that we might walk on it and thus reach the island. The pipe was narrow, made slippery by the rain, the turbid waters of the Potomac were uninviting. We never winced, and said: "Let us." We had our recompense; our leader relented, and seeing in the distance a man in a boat, signed to him. The boat was as muddy and leaky as one could wish; we stood in it with our feet in water and were rowed to the island. The President struck an attitude and passing his arm around my neck, said: "Washington and Rochambeau crossing the Delaware."[29]

Although it's tantalizing to consider this humorous account a potential visit to Theodore Roosevelt Island—and it could be—I think it's more likely that President Roosevelt and the French Ambassador in his thrall were exploring what are today's East and West Potomac parks. East Potomac Park (or Hains Point) and West Potomac Park (including the Tidal Basin) were created from soil dredged from the river at the end of the nineteenth century in response to flooding and disease emanating from the polluted tidal marshes along the Potomac. Hains Point was an island during most of Roosevelt's administration, and additional soil was still being dredged from the river and added to the landscape. Hains Point is much closer and more accessible to the White House than what is now known as Theodore Roosevelt Island.

Speaking of Jusserand, this is as good a time as any to share a colorful passage from a 1919 biography of Roosevelt by William Roscoe Thayer about one of Jusserand's first adventures with the president:

Yesterday President Roosevelt invited me to take a promenade with him this afternoon at three. I arrived at the White House punctually, in afternoon dress and silk hat, as if we were to stroll in the Tuileries Garden or in the Champs Elysees. To my surprise, the President soon joined me in a tramping suit, with knickerbockers and thick boots, and soft felt hat, much worn. Two or three other gentlemen came, and we started off at what seemed to me a breakneck pace, which soon brought us out of the city. On reaching the country, the President went pell-mell over the fields, following neither road nor path, always on, on, straight ahead! I was much winded, but I would not give in, nor ask him to slow up, because I had the honor of La belle France in my heart. At last we came to the bank of a stream, rather wide and too deep to be forded. I sighed relief, because I thought that now we had reached our goal and would rest a moment and catch our breath, before turning homeward. But judge of my horror when I saw the President unbutton his clothes and heard him say, "We had better strip, so as not to wet our things in the Creek." Then I, too, for the honor of France, removed my apparel, everything except my lavender kid gloves. The President cast an inquiring look at these as if they, too, must come off, but I quickly forestalled any remark by saying, "With your permission, Mr. President, I will keep these on, otherwise it would be embarrassing if we should meet ladies." And so we jumped into the water and swam across.[30]

Thayer, an early biographer who was a friend of Roosevelt, may have taken some liberties with the narrative. According to both Roosevelt and Jusserand, the swimming portion of this event more likely took place in the Potomac River near Chain Bridge (not far upriver from Theodore Roosevelt Island). However, Jusserand did keep his lavender kid gloves on during the episode, and Gifford Pinchot, the first chief of the US Forest Service in the Roosevelt administration, and another Roosevelt adventure companion, referred to Jusserand afterwards as "the man who wore gloves while swimming."[31]

As we walked along the island trails on our far tamer adventure, Sam Sharp had his clippers at the ready, and he deftly clipped the invasive woody vines and shrubs he saw along our route. While walking through the zone where Rod and I had noted the bush honeysuckle removal, I talked to the Friends about their invasives program.

"We are focusing on shrubs and vines now and will tackle other invasives later in collaboration with the National Park Service," said Sam.

This is how things work in Rock Creek Park too. The budget-strapped NPS works with non-profit organizations and their trained volunteers to tackle the serious problem of invasives.

When we arrived at Georgetown Rock, Winthrop wandered south along the shore and then came back to lead us to a great blue heron that was standing nearly motionless in a mudflat near the rocky shore, the breeze ruffling his or her feathers. After admiring the heron, we looped back past the tall bitternut hickory and onto the swamp boardwalk, where the maples were blooming.

Midway into the swamp, we noticed fluffy cattail seeds lying on the boardwalk. Several of us bent down to pick them up and they alit from our open palms, lighter than air, the breeze carrying them up and away in small tufts.

I challenged everyone to close their eyes while holding the cattail seeds, asking them: "With eyes closed could you tell that you are holding anything at all in your hand?"

None of us could, and our murmured expressions of awe followed the cattail seeds into the air. The ingenious ways of seeds: sometimes captive in durable protective capsules; sometimes encased temporarily in tempting fruit; sometimes lighter than the air that carries them off to distant homes.

As we walked back to our cars, I absorbed a wealth of

information about the island and its history from Nicole and Sam, and Sam followed our visit up by sending me some historical documents. Nicole said that the 1st United States Colored Troops were stationed on the island during the Civil War, partially because they weren't welcomed in a DC neighborhood near Union Station. She said the island was also a station on the Underground Railroad. Nicole suggested that I tap into the archives at the Theodore Roosevelt Center at Dickinson State University in North Dakota to learn more about the island's history. I have been delving into their extensive and user-friendly digital archives.

Nicole also told me that the fiftieth anniversary of the Roosevelt sculpture and surrounding plaza is coming up in October, and she asked me if I would lead a nature walk on that day. I immediately agreed, and I have since committed to leading two summer walks and a paddling trip for the Friends of Theodore Roosevelt Island.

I also learned a daunting bit of information from Nicole: The Theodore Roosevelt Island parking lot will be closed for the foreseeable future during construction.

Tomorrow I'm leading a tour of the Capitol grounds for the US Botanic Garden. I led another USBG tour of the Capitol's historic and international trees two days ago, when the high temperature for the day was a record-tying 80 degrees (26C).

"This is the earliest spring I've seen in 40 years of visiting the Capitol," I told tree-tour participants as we walked among the Japanese flowering star and saucer magnolias.

Last night it snowed—a mere dusting—and temperatures won't get out of the 30s Fahrenheit (maximum 4C) today or tomorrow. Two tree-tours, three days apart, with a 50-degree difference in temperatures, plus a drought. Is it too much to hope for weather normalcy and appreciable precipitation of any kind?

March 8th: An Early Spring Has Come to the Island

While the thermometer ricochets from the 30s to the 80s (from around 0 to 26C), and Washington continues in a state of drought, spring inches forward, with flowers blooming two to three or even four weeks ahead of schedule.

I remarked to a field-trip group on a recent walk in Rock Creek Park: "This crazy weather is turning us all into anxious phenologists."

Phenology is the science of timing in nature: when trees leaf out, when flowers bloom to coincide with the life cycles of their pollinators, when birds migrate and nest, and so on. There are always seasonal aberrations, and nature's creatures are remarkably adaptable. However, since the end of the last Ice Age approximately 10,000 years ago, Earth has enjoyed a fairly stable climate.

When I drove through the city on Monday afternoon, March 6th, I witnessed frozen brown blooms on many early Asian magnolias. Every early-flowering magnolia around the White House was an ugly brown, which seemed dismally symbolic. Some of the early-flowering cherry blossoms were also looking limp and brownish. Coaxed into blooming too early by record high temperatures, they couldn't withstand the freeze that followed. The little star magnolia we admired in bloom on last Wednesday's tour of the Capitol grounds looked scraggly and stressed during the Saturday tour.

In addition to many serious regional and global concerns, climate change presents deep challenges on the heart level. I am emotionally tuned to the dramatic changes that each of the four distinct seasons brings. No seasonal transformation is more ingrained in my heart than the hope of spring after a long, cold winter. But, when winter has barely hinted at the need for hibernation, how can I wholeheartedly long for warmth and verdancy, or welcome it with open arms when it arrives too soon? When drought is factored in with wild swings in heat and cold, when the flowers are stressed and confused and the spring peepers have no ponds in which to breed, how can I surrender to the joy unique to spring in the temperate zone? These are questions that trouble me deeply, especially when I ask them of myself indoors.

Then I find myself walking across a footbridge to an island. Wood ducks and common mergansers are splashing in Little River, and I see maples and elms blooming along the island shore. Grandmother is as magnificently white and beckoning as ever, leaning far out over Roosevelt Rock, and is that a yellow haze of spicebush blooms glowing in the lower canopy? The climate may be in serious jeopardy the world over, and a president who denies our impact on it may occupy a White House surrounded by frozen brown magnolias a mile and a half away, but can I deny the happy reality of the outgoing tide and the setting sun? I cannot!

Early Monday evening, joy took hold of my anxious heart as I walked across the bridge and stepped foot on the island. I was greeted by galaxies of delicate pink and white star-shaped spring beauty blossoms, triumphing in the continuous carpet of invasive lesser celandine leaves. The little spring beauties with their shocking pink anthers and peppermint candy-striped petals cheered me with their adaptability.

Years ago, I wondered why, when all the other early-spring ephemerals had ceased to bloom, in late April or so, the spring beauties went on and on, even as the canopy began seriously leafing out above them, the common cue to desist blooming for the early woodland wildflowers. My botanist friend Cris Fleming solved the mystery for me, and I was a little embarrassed by its obviousness. The spring beauties went on blooming because each flower was attached to an elongated cluster called a raceme, and the raceme bloomed from the bottom up, with individual flowers staggered in their blooming times. So small and tightly wound are the racemes that you really have to get down on the forest floor to see what's happening!

I began my last book ten winters ago when Jim and I were

alarmed to see spring beauties in bud on New Year's Day, more than two months ahead of their normal blooming time. They were budding on the heels of an abnormally warm December, during which daffodils bloomed at Christmas in Washington. That year, on a mid-January field trip I led for the Audubon Naturalist Society in Rock Creek Park, they were fully out. Since then I've seen the little spring beauties bloom early and late, depending on our now wildly variable winters, and I've come to believe that nothing seems to faze them. Unlike the highly ephemeral flowers of the bloodroot or the rare twinleaf, which can get easily zapped by an untimely 80-degree (26C) day, the spring beauties, delicate as they may appear, seem to be obstinately adaptable.

As I moseyed along in their good company, my eyes and ears were drawn toward the river, where the incoming tide was high and crew teams were out in force from Thompson Boat Center to Key Bridge, as sure a sign of spring as anything of the natural world. Aren't we humans happiest, I mused, when we are part of nature, in harmony with the seasons and tides, rather than apart or opposed? When Roosevelt was a boy, he spent hours alone in his boat on Long Island's Oyster Bay, and he rowed on the Charles when he was at Harvard. I could imagine him happily soaking up the scene before my eyes.

The next day, I met Betsy Lovejoy and Joanna Sturm on the footbridge at noon. As I approached the bridge, my friends were watching wood ducks and a female merganser through their binoculars as a stiff breeze blew. When we stepped onto the island they were enchanted by all the flowers and fruits of our early spring: the abundant dangling clusters of little green elm samaras, each about half-grown, with a seed in the middle of the encircling papery wing, a wing that on close examination was fringed with silky white hairs; the yellow haze of spicebush flowers adorning spicy-fragrant twigs; the silver and red maple flowers, and of course the spring beauties in all their starry profusion. I got out my hand lens to get a close look at the spring beauty petals, anthers, and three-parted pistil, and Betsy used her binoculars for a close-up view. Heading north toward Grandmother, we came upon a few cut-leaved toothwort flowers that had also managed to defy the lesser celandine carpet. I showed Betsy and Joanna their four-petaled "cruciferous" flowers and deeply cut opposite and whorled leaves that look a bit like the leaves of a mind-altering herb that is now legal in many parts of the USA.

I took them to see the beaver activity near Grandmother that had captivated Joanna's distant cousin Winthrop. There were more fresh wood-chips at the base of the tulip-tree, and tracks in the adjacent mudflat.

On the northern end of the island we stumbled upon a small colony of Virginia bluebells in bud and newly blooming. While we were admiring the bluebells for their beauty and fortitude, Betsy noticed some activity in the leaf litter at the base of one of the flower clusters, and soon a sleek, striped garter snake slithered into view. Just as quickly as the snake appeared, it disappeared, so crafty and camouflaged that we couldn't figure out where it had gone. The singular magic of snakes!

After our bluebell reverie, we wandered into the swamp, where robins were wildly and melodiously singing, and out to the cypress lookout, where Joanna and I lay on our backs on the boardwalk watching the little bead-like male cones of the bald-cypresses dance in the breeze under the drifting clouds as Betsy ate her lunch. The tide was visibly rising beyond the narrow-leaved cattails.

Betsy said before we left the island, "Next time we come here together, the ospreys will be back!"

For me, that will be the best spring miracle of all, whenever it occurs. Crazily, I have no earthly idea when to expect their return.

March 15th: Winter's Return

Winter has returned with a vengeance. On a family visit to

Vermont and New Hampshire last week, the thermometer hovered at zero Fahrenheit (about -18C) on two consecutive mornings, and I finally got to see the nearly full sugar moon "on the breast of the new-fallen snow" at my sister Ellie's Vermont farmhouse.

Here at home I'm rekindling my romance with winter. I thought myself cured of winter longing, but that was a lie I'd told myself as I was desperately trying to embrace a too-early spring. However, my winter romance is tempered by concern for all the living beings who are dealing with climate extremes that threaten their breeding, leafing, blooming, and fruiting. Early this morning I woke up and surprised myself by spontaneously writing and submitting an op-ed to the *Washington Post* titled "'Phenology Anxiety' and the Cherry Blossoms." The op-ed desk wrote to tell me they had routed it to the "Close to Home" section and I'll have to wait to see if it will be accepted.

Even non-nature-oriented people are feeling anxious and disturbed. Washingtonians' allergies have kicked in early this year, and all around us we see frozen brown magnolias as we hear the news that the cherry blossoms are seriously threatened for the first time in their 105-year history. I wrote to my friend Gene Kingsbury (whose family has farmed near Sugarloaf Mountain for more than a hundred years) and yesterday he wrote back:

> We've already lost our apricots and sweet plums. Peaches have not yet bloomed, but these temps can still freeze the buds. I checked quite a few this morning and had difficulty finding live buds...and two more really cold nights on the way. Apples should be okay, but peaches are our main crop.

I have my fingers crossed for Gene's family and their orchards, and for our Tidal Basin cherry trees. In my piece, I wrote that the best remedy for worries about nature—although perhaps a bit counter-intuitive—was to immerse yourself in natural beauty, simply because I have found this to be true. Kate Maynor, Susan Austin Roth, and I exchanged concerned emails before the cold snap and snowstorm, sharing photos of bloodroot flowers and other vulnerable plants. We have jokingly called ourselves "the Babes," since a Colorado hiking trip some years ago. After our flurry of concerns and pictures had flown through cyberspace, and with the snow approaching, Susan wrote to Kate and me: "Go Babes and love Nature in all her mystery." Her words inspired me deeply, because yes, Nature is mysterious and invites our love as well as our hand-wringing.

Monday night, 24 years to the day after the big March snowstorm of 1993, the snow came. It was not impressive in amount, greatly diminished by a fair amount of sleet and freezing rain, but it did its magic trick—whitening the land and stopping all motorized traffic in our neighborhood other than plows for many hours. The flowering pear and cherry in Esther Schrader and Nick Anderson's yard across the street faded into the white landscape, and I just checked the trees and they clearly look a little worse for wear today. What I'm wondering is how plants learn. Can they learn to hold back from flowering and leafing when the Earth warms treacherously early? Or do they have to wait for the trial and error of the long haul of evolution to cope? Many of the plants that are hardest hit this year are Asian natives, and it makes sense that they would suffer the most since they evolved elsewhere.

Here I am in hand-wringing mode again, while trying to surrender to Susan's call to "love Nature in all her mystery." The day before it snowed I had walked among the budding and blooming Virginia bluebells, common blue violets, bloodroot, spring beauties, and yellow-flowering spicebush at Boundary Bridge. After the snow, all was tucked away under a layer of white with only the spicebush visible.

I'm happy to say that once I stuck the metal toe-loops of my boots in my cross-country skis and began gliding over Boundary

Bridge and into Rock Creek Park, I was deep in mystery. The skiing was perfect, fast and easy. Skiing along a flowing creek is about as good as it gets for inducing feelings of the happy, mellow, ecstatic kind. Although the bluebells were buried, I was intrigued by the emerging spring growth visible under the snow: tiny green samaras in the crowns of the American elms and on top of the snow; bursting green boxelder twigs; and the ubiquitous spicebush. Sparrows and juncos were busy feeding on the seeds and buds that had fallen on the snowy ground, and cardinals were energetically working the tops of the elm trees. The robins I'd seen foraging in the leaf litter, the day before the storm, were still out and about, although none were singing as they had on Theodore Roosevelt Island the day Betsy, Joanna, and I visited.

As I skied along a musical stretch of the creek, a great blue heron flew past me, with gray feathers a few shades darker than the cloud cover above. For the next hour I met no one on the trail, although I was following the tracks of many walkers and their dogs, and one other cross-country skier. When I reached the West Beach Drive overpass, a kingfisher flew chatteringly downstream, landing in a snag just before the bridge. She then flew under the overpass and perched in a second snag across from the mouth of Fenwick Branch. Suddenly her characteristic chatter ceased, and she dove headfirst into the creek and caught a fish!

As I followed the kingfisher to Fenwick Branch, snow started falling. It continued to fall as I skied to a skunk cabbage swamp, where green leaves were poking up through the snow. I've seen the heat-generating reddish flower spathes of skunk cabbage pierce through ice and snow during many winters, but the aesthetics of their large unfurling green leaves amid the snowy landscape were entirely new to me.

As large flakes filled the air, I skied to the edge of the creek and stood by the water for the longest time, just watching the snow fall. My body and soul settled into the remembered magic of falling snow. The quiet was disturbed not by any human-made sounds but by the loud raucous call of a pileated woodpecker. Looking up I saw a pair engaged in energetic activity around a large oval cavity of a tree next to the creek. It seemed like nesting behavior.

Watching the pileated pair in the falling snow sparked a poignant recent memory. I was the wedding officiant for a young friend and colleague in the Catoctin Mountains during the fall of 2015. Just before Stephanie and her fiancé Jimmy were due to walk down the outdoor "aisle" in the pines, a rare October snowsquall filled the air. The couple walked gamely down the aisle and up to the rustic altar where I stood waiting, holding a white shawl. I gave the shawl to Jimmy, who in the most loving, nurturing manner, draped it around Stephanie's bare shoulders. During the ceremony we were "interrupted" by another, very noisy, couple. A pair of pileated woodpeckers flew into the branches of the tree above us, where they blithely carried on to the delight of everyone in attendance, especially the loving human pair standing beneath their tree.

March 16th: Whither the Republic?

Yesterday, after writing and submitting my piece on "phenology anxiety" and recording my skiing adventure along Rock Creek, I drove to the Georgetown waterfront and crossed Key Bridge to Theodore Roosevelt Island. It was a cold, blustery day and I was warmly dressed in boots, snow pants, parka, and heavy gloves. Walking across Key Bridge, I savored the view of the island and the city beyond. The lowering sun created a peach glow in the wooded north and west, and toward the south and east, where the heart of the city lies, the snow-covered island was crowned with the brilliantly sunlit white trunks and limbs of Grandmother and her kin. Just peeking up behind the island's trees: the top of the white Lincoln Memorial. To complete the scene from the high bridge, the tide was out and the island's northern mudflats looked like a beckoning beach.

Steeped in the beauty of winter in our riverside city, I thought: Washington doesn't get enough aesthetic recognition. Pedestrians on Key Bridge are afforded fabulous Washington views. I'm sure every one of the bridges over the Potomac and Anacostia rivers provides some sort of stunning perspective when crossed on foot.

When I reached the Virginia shore, I turned left onto the Mount Vernon bike trail. I've already grown to love the walk down the switch-backing ramp of the bike trail that is my new way of reaching the island now that the parking lot is closed. From the ramp, you look directly across Little River to Grandmother and her wooded island. Rush-hour traffic was moving steadily along the George Washington Memorial Parkway, and the tall buildings of Rosslyn rose over my right shoulder. Over my left shoulder a blue-green Little River flowed past the snow-covered island at low tide with mudflats growing ever pinker in the setting sun. At my feet was a bike path rutted with frozen snow.

Along the sides of the bike path, sparrows were pecking at a supper of seeds that had fallen from the trees. They hopped across the ground leaving no tracks on the frozen snow as they dined on fallen elm samaras and the tiny achenes of sycamores whose fruiting balls had begun to break up in the March wind. The snow was decorated with the dry and tiny cylindrical sycamore fruits with their splayed parachuting hairs attached.

I ran into only a couple of hardy souls on bicycles as I approached the island on the bike path. I watched the cyclists' tires wobbling on the rutted icy path as they clutched their handlebars to stay aright. I surmised that these were a handful of the serious daily commuters I often see here and on the Capital Crescent Trail.

There were no vehicles in the closed parking lot, with only fencing, some sandbags along the water, and a lone porta potty to indicate a construction site.

The sun was lowering as I stepped onto the footbridge to the island. Conventional wisdom may have argued against crossing the icy bridge with no flashlight, no working cellphone (my battery was dead), and probably no other person on the island. But conventional wisdom is one of the niggling aspects of modern life that Nature so blithely sweeps aside.

I crossed the cold waters of Little River, which bore no icy edges, thanks to the precipitousness of winter's return after seasonally abnormal heat. The spicebushes and silver maples next to the bridge were in bloom, the yellow of the little spicebush flowers brilliant against the snowy landscape, the twigs emitting an especially sharp and pleasing fragrance into the cold air. The elm twigs were heavy with little green samaras.

I held onto the railing of the bridge to walk across the last few feet before the island. I was traversing a frozen jumble of footprints. Many people had been to the island since the snow, which warmed my heart. Those many people also seemed to have left, which warmed my heart further. I breathed deeply and gratefully when I realized that I was probably the only person on the island. At that moment an airplane flew overhead, reminding me that just recently no planes had flown.

The island was encased in a thick sheet of frozen snow. If I was to continue to the interior, which I felt compelled to do, I would have to figure out a way to skate over the frozen ground. I found that my clunky thick-soled hiking boots actually functioned surprisingly well as skates.

The sheen of the snow uplifted my spirits as I skated around TR's plaza toward the hill above the swamp. The footprints of adults and children were poignantly interspersed, and I could picture the giddy youngsters finally getting a chance to stomp through some snow after our strange winter. At the eastern edge of the plaza, the footprints broke through to the pebbled ground underneath, affording me some traction. When I reached the Upland Trail I stopped to absorb the eloquence of the moment. Black-branched trees lined the whitened path that held the footprints of all those island visitors who came to enjoy the island after the snow despite the lack of parking. Their footprints trailed north toward the bluebells that I hoped would re-emerge after snow melt. The sky was a deepening blue with pink clouds along the horizon behind the tall trees.

I crossed the trail and scooted down the icy hill toward the swamp on my butt as it was the only way to go. I sat for a while at the base of a hickory tree and enjoyed the cold and quiet between planes. No spring peepers called from the swamp as they had on a warmer February evening when I sat under the same tree.

I climbed back up the hill to TR's plaza, holding onto the trunks of young trees for leverage. When I got back to the plaza, I found a question scrawled in the snow with a large stick and frozen in place: *Whither the Republic?* It was not far from the "Youth" tablet with its engraved quote about character.

I walked away from the question written in the snow, but the words stayed with me as I stood at the edge of the plaza looking at Roosevelt with his right arm upstretched. Whither the Republic?—a silent plea more powerful than a chorus of protest chants.

There was a long cessation of overhead planes and unbroken quiet but for the chirping birds, who were foraging for seeds on top of the frozen snow all around the statue. And to take the serenity of the moment right over the top, a white-throated sparrow whistled a fragment of his penetrating song.

As I walked back across the footbridge to Virginia and then crossed Key Bridge to Washington in the dark, I thought about TR's fearless love, not only of democratic freedoms and responsibilities, but also of adventure. I'm reading *River of Doubt*, about his post-Bull Moose campaign expedition down the uncharted waters of an Amazon tributary that brought him perilously close to death. I thought about his hunting expedition in Africa, and his move to the Dakota badlands as a young man. Closer to home, I mused about his 12-mile tramps through Rock Creek Park and his fearless rock scrambling. TR was a seriously asthmatic child who learned to take life head on, with the support of his loving but demanding father.

I couldn't help but think about how tame my own life's adventures have been. Should I challenge myself with some serious adventure? In the wake of my deeply restorative island winter walk and the glow of its aftermath, I wonder.

Theodore Roosevelt, your legacy has inspired me. I'm reminded of your "Citizenship in a Republic" speech that you gave in Paris after your African trip. You are often quoted from that speech about the "man in the arena," who, "if he fails, at least fails while daring greatly, so that his place shall never be with those cold and timid souls who neither know victory nor defeat."[32] There was a direct connection between your fearlessness in the field and your daring on the national political stage. I wish to emulate your courageous approach in all of my own arenas. May we all.

March 22nd: Spring Equinox

Two days ago, we celebrated the spring equinox, time of equal day and night from the equator to the poles. My friends Anne Sturm and Ellen Gordon held a celebration on Sugarloaf Mountain for many of those who had gathered on the little mountain for the winter solstice. I was with them in spirit as I remained home at my laptop putting the spit and polish on edits of my piece on "phenology anxiety," which will go online at washingtonpost. com on Friday the 24th and will appear in Sunday's paper.

On the political front, it is too difficult to keep up with the actions Trump is taking to gut environmental policy and all the other protective measures I care deeply about, or to keep pace with his insane tweeting. I keep as current as possible, but I've got to live my life. This new balancing act is a topic of conversation that comes up constantly among my friends and colleagues.

I hope that with passionate activism and the deliberateness of the courts we can slow down Trump's initiatives enough to minimize the damage. However, should a terrorist attack on our homeland or a world military crisis occur, all bets are off. "Will we survive Donald Trump?" is a question haunting many minds. Whither the Republic?

March 29th: A Visit to Pittsburgh

I'm sitting across from Sophie in her neighborhood coffee shop in Pittsburgh. A sign on the door reads: "Pittsburgh, City of Bridges, all are welcome here, this is a hate-free zone." All around the neighborhood, homes sport green, blue, and orange signs reading: "No matter where you are from, we're glad you're our neighbor" in Spanish, English, and Arabic.

Sophie will join the University of Pittsburgh faculty in the fall and I'm staying with her in her apartment in a Tudor-style home.

Sophie's guest bedroom seems to invite deep evocative dreaming. I awoke the first morning I was here, recovering from a powerful and disturbing dream. In the dream I was in front of a large brick building when some policemen arrested and handcuffed two young men who I assumed had committed a crime. Then they arrested another pair of young men. This process was repeated several times, and I realized that these were immigrants who were being rounded up for deportation. Each time the young men were handcuffed, I could see the looks of resignation on their faces. Many of them looked into my eyes. One young man was wearing an adult uniform yet he had the face of an innocent-looking boy.

As I realized what was happening, I began to sob uncontrollably and tried to figure out what to do. I woke up as I was sobbingly following the parade of handcuffed young men up a long hill, thinking maybe if I followed there would be something I could do to help them.

Whither the Republic?

Just as I typed that question, John Lennon's "Imagine" began playing here in the coffee shop.

My op-ed piece was posted on washingtonpost.com Friday evening, and by the next morning there were numerous websites that had picked it up. Today, five days later, "phenology anxiety" is a thing on the internet. Almost instantly, responses came trickling in, at first mostly from people I had forwarded the piece to via email. The title of the online piece: "Worried About the Cherry Blossoms? You May Have 'Phenology Anxiety.'"

I went down to the Tidal Basin that evening to see how the cherry blossoms were faring, and my heart swelled with poignant joy when I saw their ethereal magic springing forth after the freeze that blighted as many as half their buds. As I walked around the basin in the dark, a beaver came swimming along beside me and we moved in tandem for a time.

Just after seeing the beaver I received an email from Wendy, who said she loved the piece and she was sharing it with a wide circle of friends. When I told her about the beaver, she wrote: "Uh-oh. It won't be long for this world if it starts chopping down cherry trees."

"Go back to the river," I mentally urged the beaver as I remembered a cherry-chopping incident years ago, after which beavers were trapped and relocated.

Once the piece appeared on the local opinions page of the Sunday paper, emails from friends and colleagues began pouring in. Readers resonated with the sentiments I expressed, especially the lines in the closing paragraph:

I've found that the most effective remedy for phenology anxiety is to immerse myself in the natural beauty in and around our city. The more intimately I know our wild back yard, the more deeply I appreciate the dependence of trees, wildflowers, birds and all flora and fauna on the endlessly variable but so far reliable seasons. And with familiarity comes the desire to protect.[33]

Friends wrote about the miracle of finding one or two living blossoms on a frozen magnolia. They wrote about goldfinches turning from green to yellow with the spring, about the calls of returning phoebes and choruses of spring peepers. My friend Bev Thoms, who lives near Sugarloaf Mountain, described spring unfolding in her yard, including phoebe nest-building under the eaves of her house. She wrote: "I am anxious about climate-change impacts on our earth, and rejoice at the little signs that life is persisting."

Nature may be feeling the pinch of our resource-reckless ways, but we are but a part of the great mystery connecting all precious and interdependent life. Whenever we take time from our busy lives to tune in to the wonders around us, our hearts open and remind us that this is so.

On Sunday, March 26th, a gray cold day in the 40s (around 4–9C) after a warm one in the 70s (21–26C), I bundled up in layers and set off on my bike for Theodore Roosevelt Island and the Tidal Basin. My dad, who had just celebrated his eighty-ninth birthday skiing the black diamond slopes at Okemo in Vermont, followed by two tense days at the hospital with my mom who was undergoing tests (all thankfully negative), wrote to me: "I'm delighting in picturing you on your bike headed for the Tidal Basin—just like Louis Halle 72 years ago. And from what I can glean, in similar weather!"

Louis Halle was a state department employee, who, during 1945, the final year of World War II, took it upon himself to monitor the unfolding spring, leading to his book *Spring in Washington*, a local classic. He biked through Rock Creek Park and along the Potomac River, often at dawn, describing the details of weather, ice melting on the river, the winter birds, and then the return of migrants through and to the Washington region. He waxed philosophical about life and how humans shelter themselves in what he called "the hive" where they miss Nature's dramas. I have been trying to read along with Halle in real time, comparing where we are today weather-wise with where we were then.

My 17-year-old dad lived in Washington during the spring of 1945 while his father held a position with the Office of Strategic Services (OSS), so this book has always held a special place in his heart. When I moved to Washington at the age of 25, my dad gave me the book as a gift and it helped inspire me to write the first edition of *City of Trees*. Later, when *Spring in Washington* had gone out of print, I suggested that my then-publisher, Johns Hopkins, reissue it. I don't know if my recommendation had much influence, but Hopkins did publish the book and, in a bit of full-circle synchronicity, the original hardcover had a blurb about *City of Trees* on the book jacket.

I have grown fond of the bike trip to Theodore Roosevelt Island, my initial destination on Sunday. I biked down the Capital Crescent Trail, took some steps up to the C&O Canal as I neared Georgetown, and then crossed the canal on a pedestrian/bike ramp. I walked my bike across Key Bridge, and when I reached the empty island parking lot, I was heartened to see redbuds with emerging flower buds up and down their twigs and branches, and the whitened limbs of Grandmother and her sycamore clan beyond the green river. I crossed the footbridge to the island, where the spicebush was a vibrant yellow under the thick cloud cover and the silver maple samaras were beginning to form, in company with the elm samaras still on the trees. A naturalized flowering crabapple bore pink buds, with a few opening to five white petals.

As I walked north along the western shoreline, I found spring beauties that had re-emerged after the icy grip of accumulated sleet and snow. Their blossoms were nodding and mostly closed on this cold gray day. Why risk exposing precious reproductive parts when no pollinators are out and about? The lesser celandine leaf carpet was as thick and impenetrable-looking as ever, but here and there a speckled trout-lily leaf sliced through it, and the occasional cluster of cut-leaved toothwort and a few common blue violets were also up and blooming after the snow.

The "beaver" tree, a fairly tall tulip-tree near Grandmother, is now almost fully girdled by our flat-tailed furry friends, but its buds were beginning to break. And near Grandmother, I found some clusters of Virginia bluebells, their pink buds opening to bell-shaped, nodding pale blue flowers. The larger clusters of bluebells at the northern end of the island were blooming profusely, the only sign of wear and tear from snow and freeze being a slightly burnt look along the tops of some of their leaves, like the edges of old-fashioned parchment.

When I reached Georgetown Rock, a great blue heron flapped its long cloud-gray wings as it flew downriver. The buds of the blackhaw viburnum were breaking, and when I looked closely at these small trees with their "alligator" bark, I saw charming round clusters of tight flower buds amid the tiny emergent leaves. Nearby, the bladdernuts were in the early stages of budbreak, and the non-native honeysuckles were well along in the leafing process.

The boardwalk was littered with half-grown silver maple samaras. Up in the trees three squirrels were in a feasting frenzy, flinging stray winged seeds in all directions. I had to retrace my steps and leave the island so that I could make it to the Tidal Basin and back home before dark. One brave little spring peeper was testing the afternoon air.

I rode down the Mount Vernon trail toward Memorial Bridge and over the Boundary Channel, a path I hadn't followed on my bike in many years. As I pedaled under flowering maples and greening weeping willows, I thought of George Washington, who wrote on this very date in 1786 (and I quoted him in my op-ed piece in the *Post* exactly 231 years later):

> The warmth of yesterday and this day, forwarded vegetation much; the buds of some trees, particularly the Weeping Willow and Maple, had displayed their leaves & blossoms and all others were swelled, and many ready to put forth. The apricot trees were beginning to blossom and the grass to shew its verdure.[34]

I thought of Thomas Jefferson and his weather diary and how both men, passionate farmers, horticulturists, and naturalists, who dearly loved their own land and all of wild and cultivated America, differed from the current resident of the White House, who relates to the earth from a Trump Tower window or the putting green.

I pedaled down to Memorial Bridge, through Lady Bird Johnson Park, where daffodils were blooming. I stopped at a plaque that read:

> The dogwood and daffodil plantings on this island are dedicated to President and Mrs. Lyndon B. Johnson who challenged America to make more beautiful the environment of all of its citizens. (1968)

I rode my bike over Memorial Bridge toward the Lincoln Memorial and from there to the Tidal Basin. The cherries were fully out, their ethereal magic bearing no visible scars from the previous weeks' hot and cold tug of war. Trees young and old grew side by side—gnarled 105-year-olds next to smooth-barked 10-year-olds—all sending forth blossoms forming a continuous pale pink cloud. Throngs crowded the basin, smiling and snapping pictures as they passed under the flowering boughs. The cherry trees had pulled off their magic act once again.

Chapter Ten

April—An Island in Bloom

April 6th: A Flowering Orgy at the Island

Theodore Roosevelt Island is spilling over with spring wildflowers. From the moment I step off the footbridge and onto the island, I'm greeted by the galaxy of earth-hugging candy-striped spring beauty flowers, their faces lifted toward the sun. Colonies of nodding trout-lilies with swept back yellow "tepals" (petals and petaloid sepals) above pairs of basal leaves speckled like brook trout spring forth in their midst. These trout-lily colonies can be up to 300 years old, reaching back to Nacotchtank times. Native violets hug the ground in charming groups. An occasional cluster of taller cut-leaved toothwort with four-parted pale pink flowers and deeply cut leaves rises above the spring beauty multitudes. As I walk toward the northern shore, islands of Virginia bluebells tremble in the breeze, their nodding blue bells interspersed with unopened pink buds. Heart-shaped leaves of wild ginger lie close to the ground, small burgundy flowers hiding beneath them. Peering inside each one is like looking into a miniature domed cathedral. Another burgundy flower is blooming in a small cluster nearby—a sessile or toad-shade trillium, with three-petaled flowers and spotted leaves.

How Theodore Roosevelt would rejoice to see his memorial island in full flower today! In his 1913 autobiography he professed his love for wildflowers, writing:

> Long Island [location of Roosevelt's beloved home, Sagamore Hill] is not as rich in flowers as the valley of the Hudson. Yet there are many. Early in April there is one hillside near us which glows like a tender flame with the white of the bloodroot. About the same time we find the shy mayflower, the trailing arbutus; and although we rarely pick wild flowers, one member of the household always plucks a little bunch of mayflowers to send to a friend working in Panama, whose soul hungers for the Northern spring. Then there are shadblow [also called shadbush and serviceberry] and delicate anemones, about the time of the cherry blossoms; the brief glory of the apple orchards follows; and then the thronging dogwoods fill the forests with their radiance; and so flowers follow flowers until the springtime splendor closes with the laurel and the evanescent, honey-sweet locust bloom. The late summer flowers follow, the flaunting lilies, and cardinal flowers, and marshmallows, and pale beach rosemary; and the goldenrod and the asters when the afternoons shorten and we again begin to think of fires in the wide fireplaces.[35]

Nearing Georgetown Rock on Roosevelt's memorial island, an occasional slender rock-cress plant blooms with small white four-petaled flowers, and, at the rock itself, trout-lily and spring beauty spring from the crevices of the rocky Piedmont's last eastern gasp, exhibiting the power of the deceptively delicate-looking plant life of earliest spring. Lesser celandine rules at the northern edge of the swamp, but as I walk down the boardwalk, taller golden ragwort and white-flowered spring cress—both native—spring forth in delightful clumps. Ancient-lineaged horsetail, a relative of the ferns, grows next to the boardwalk, like a tiny bamboo forest with a feathery canopy.

And the trees. I've visited the island three times this week, and in a succession of days I've glimpsed the magic of budbreak. I met botany buddy Elizabeth Rives, who is just back from wintering in New Zealand, at the island on Tuesday to scout for a field trip we led yesterday (Wednesday). On Tuesday, the witch-hazel leaves were emerging in pairs, their tiny blades held tight together in prayer position. Yesterday, less than 24 hours later, as we led our Audubon Naturalist Society group from the footbridge toward the northern island shore, the pairs of leaves, all shiny and newborn green with richly textured veins, had doubled in size and they were opening to the spring sun.

The tall oaks were tipped with gold, their dangling clusters of male catkins dancing on the light spring wind. You could walk under them without giving them a glance, curse the catkins as they land on your windshield, or you could, as we did, look up in awed amazement at the golden-crowned trees under the blue spring sky. Oak flowers are wind pollinated so they need no show of colorful, fragrant petals. The female flowers are so tiny they can't be seen from the ground with the naked eye, but up close they look like miniature versions of the acorns they will become. The beauty of an oak in bloom, because of the male catkins, is astonishing if you know how to see it.

Yesterday we examined the purply pink flowers of the redbud, and I showed them the five individual petals of each tiny blossom like the ones of last summer's groundnut that I witnessed from my kayak: the two lower petals fused to form a protective "keel," the upstanding "banner" in the back, and the two side "wings." We looked at several beech trees, some with a few buds still slender and sharply pointed as in winter, and most with many bulging, white-tipped buds, the silky hairs of the imminently birthing leaves spilling from their tops.

Some of the bursting sycamore buds were dripping sap, and some were already revealing tight round clusters of flowers in bud or tiny leaves. Male cottonwoods displayed their almost indecently red caterpillar-like catkins, and the females bore catkins of a more chaste-looking green.

Yesterday, our field-trip group picnicked on the bald-cypress platform. Those deciduous conifers, which still held their bead-like strands of male cones, were just beginning to sport tiny needles, still merely knobby clusters for the most part. The tide was low low low and still visibly outgoing. The day before, when Elizabeth and I were scouting for the field trip, the island was flooded after the recent spring rains. Small fish swam in places that were usually dry land, and wood ducks were paddling far inland in flooded temporary pools.

By yesterday, the floods were a memory. I ate my lunch facing east, the tidal inlet to my back. Midway into our picnic lunch my friend Allen Browne exclaimed, "Look! The tide has changed direction and is now coming in." Although I felt sorry to have missed my chance to see the tide reverse, I was awed by how swiftly it flowed in a reverse direction and how quickly the water covered the mudflats and began to engulf the cypress knees.

Looking west across the inlet I saw a row of leafing tulip-trees on the wooded hillside, and two sassafras trees sporting small yellow flowers. I pointed them out and told the group as we were packing up after lunch: "Sassafras is in the same plant family as the ubiquitous spicebush: the laurel family of Old World laurel-crown fame, which also claims culinary delights cinnamon, bay leaf, and avocado." And I added something that many of them already knew: "Sassafras roots once flavored root beer and they are still used to make tea in Appalachia."

Before we began our walk back to the footbridge, we watched

a pair of birds energetically building a nest and lining it with cattail fluff. We had several enthusiastic birders in our group but no experts. The group consensus, after a little speculation, was that the pair were blue-gray gnatcatchers. We are supposed to get some strong storms today and I'm thinking about that nest and hoping it holds.

April 12th: Lost Atlantis Found

Lately Theodore Roosevelt Island has felt like the lost continent of Atlantis as it's been so hard to reach given my schedule. Yesterday I drove to the mouth of Rock Creek where a tour I'm giving for Smithsonian Associates will commence two days from now. The Potomac was filled with high-school crew teams. When I noticed a couple of kayaks on the water, a lightbulb switched on in my head. Thompson Boat Center must be open a few days shy of the official opening date of April 15th.

Within minutes I was wearing a life jacket, with paddle in hand and binoculars around my neck, as I waited at the dock for one of the boathouse staff to help me into my first kayak of the season.

My spirits soared once I was out on the river, with crew teams headed north and south, a Washington water taxi drifting by, ring-billed gulls overhead, and sleek black cormorants whizzing past and landing in the river. There was a breeze and a pretty good chop to the water as I paddled toward the eastern shore of the island.

Virginia bluebells bloomed at the edge of the forest, their sunlit blossoms the color of the spring sky. The woods were seriously greening up, the graceful dangling clusters of boxelder flowers joined by small tri- and five-parted leaves. A wood duck pair paddled to the shore next to me and then traversed a glistening sandy mudflat on their matching orange legs, the male's feathers and bill an improbable tapestry of green, red, chestnut, black, and white, the gray-brown female sporting her white eyeliner. This pair will probably nest in a riverside tree, and when their ducklings are a day old they will jump from the nest—perhaps with a parental nudge—soaring as much as 30 feet to the ground where they will splash into the Potomac, or land on dry land, bouncing like tennis balls. Day-old wood ducks have been known to march up to a mile to reach the water with their parents.

Perhaps because recent world events give my thoughts a pre-apocalyptic bent, I have become enamored of the form of every living thing, especially birds. An individual bird, any bird, is such a miracle of nature. Louis Halle's birds of record, in *Spring in Washington* in 1945, are no longer here along the Potomac, but their descendants, many generations later, are still residing here or returning from parts south to make their nests along Washington's shores. Individual birds are mortal, yet the perfect form of each bird species lives on.

Isn't that the primal appeal of the Noah's Ark story? The magic of two by two? All the living forms, each so remarkably individual, holding the promise of their uniqueness for time immemorial? The pair representing all that is to come, lifting us above the anguish and uncertainty of the present moment.

I paddled down to Little Island, anxiously scanning the skies and trees for ospreys. Each time I tried to turn a soaring gull into a soaring osprey, I had to face the fact that this isn't how it works. You can't will an osprey. That particular form of bird will keep me waiting and hoping for another day.

Shag Island was its usual haven for cormorants, as were the surrounding waters. I wanted to paddle around to the inlet between Little Island and TRI, but sediment had piled up all around it, and with the tide pretty low, there was no getting near the shore.

On my way back to the boathouse I had an inspiration. I *could* get to the island on foot. All I had to do was dock my boat on a mudflat and step ashore. As I paddled up to a good landing spot,

I noticed how much new trash, including some large blue barrels, had accrued since the spring floods. I tried to channel Leonard Cohen's Suzanne to help me focus on beauty over garbage. That worked pretty well, but once ashore I needed more inspiration to focus on the bluebells rather than the lesser celandine.

I could see the boardwalk ahead of me, across a shiny green-yellow speckled carpet of celandine with triumphant clumps of bluebells prevailing. I walked up to the boardwalk hoping I was near the gnatcatcher nest so that I could tell if it had survived the recent storm. I wasn't sure if I should go left or right on the boardwalk, and the clock was nearing six, the kayak witching hour. I had to give up on the nest for now, content in the knowledge that Atlantis was not lost after all.

April 17th: Fire, Rain, and Lilacs at the Ashby Inn

A light, sweet, slanting rain is falling on the apple blossoms, lilacs, dogwoods, and tulips in the village of Paris, Virginia and the greening pastures and Blue Ridge Mountains surrounding it. The windows of our room in the Ashby Inn are thrown open to the songs of white-throated sparrows, robins, and red-winged blackbirds as a fire simmers in the fireplace. I've drawn my comfy chair close to the fire where I've propped my laptop on a flowered pillow. My bare feet rest on the warm stones of the hearth, which holds a single lilac cluster (plucked in the rain) in a Fiji water bottle. I'm brewing ginger-pear tea.

After an intense work week for both of us, Jim and I decided to splurge on a short getaway to our favorite Virginia refuge. It's Monday morning and Jim has left for work. I have the day here alone and I plan to hike up through Sky Meadows to the Appalachian Trail once the rain stops. For now, I'm basking in a reverie of fire, rain, and lilacs.

I concluded my all-day bus tour through Rock Creek Park for Smithsonian Associates on Friday with a reading of the Robert Frost poem "Nothing Gold Can Stay."

Nature's first green is gold,
Her hardest hue to hold.
Her early leaf's a flower;
But only so an hour.
Then leaf subsides to leaf.
So Eden sank to grief,
So dawn goes down to day.
Nothing gold can stay.[36]

All during the tour, I tried to convey the magic of spring's first golden blush and impress upon our participants the ephemeral tenderness of its beauty. Redbuds and dogwoods adorned the stream valley, where the trees put forth their hardest hues to hold. I know the group enjoyed seeing the migrating alewives near the Peirce Mill fish ladder and the dramatic displays of Virginia bluebells and mayapples at Boundary Bridge. But did they get the timely magic of the gold? Perhaps it requires a Vermont childhood or six decades of closely observing spring in the forest to truly appreciate the short-lived golds of April.

After the phenology anxiety of our weird winter and early spring, accompanied by news that migrating woodcocks were starving for lack of food in New England, the burgeoning of a familiar green and gold April pulls at my heart strings. Wildflowers and wood ducks on the island, alewives returning from the ocean to spawn in Rock Creek, the improbably green pastures filled with grazing cows here in Paris—the whole spring pageant is music to my ears and heart.

Last evening, as Jim and I gazed at the stars from our inn room balcony, a spring peeper chorus traveling up from the valley below, we agreed that this Easter Sunday/DC Emancipation Day was one of the happiest days we'd spent in our 43 years together. We hiked the Appalachian Trail through a tapestry of spring wildflowers, from the Thompson Wildlife Management Area to Manassas Gap, then drove up to Skyline Drive.

Shenandoah National Park was bathed in April evening sunshine, its lower slopes flowering and leafing out in Frost's hardest-to-hold hues, the upper elevations still lacking leaves. Just past Dickey Ridge we came upon a car stopped in the middle of the road, always a promising sign on Skyline Drive. And sure enough, there was a very large healthy-looking black bear appearing to pose mid-stride, with right foreleg and left hind leg at opposing angles. While we watched, the bear silently watched us, and then slowly turned around and catwalked along a fallen tree, looking for all the world like a big bear version of black tailless Balsam down to the slight swagger.

This bear didn't look like a hibernation-starved individual who had just emerged from the cave, but like a honey- and ant-fed specimen in the flush of fullest well-being.

As we drove back through the darkening hills, past Linden and Markham to Paris, each pond sending up a new wave of spring peeper song, we were heartened by the memory of the wild bear and his home in the mountains. As the night deepened during our drive, I said a silent prayer for the bear and all the ursine generations to come.

April 19th: Peppermint Flowers

Little River was high, blue-green, and as expansive-looking as a New Hampshire lake as I walked down the Mount Vernon Trail through the blooming redbuds and deep pink double-blossomed Japanese Kwanzan cherries (a tree that blooms ten days to two weeks later than the Tidal Basin Yoshino) to reach the footbridge to the island. Crews were hard at work in the parking lot, and I had to cross fresh glistening tar before stepping onto the footbridge to the island.

Once out over the water, I could feel my blood pressure and cortisol levels drop as I took in the view of the greening island and the spires of Georgetown crowning the city hills beyond. I was meeting two members of the Kingfisher Court, Betsy and

Sharon, on this April day. Betsy was somewhere on the island already, having run more than 4 miles from her home at the edge of Rock Creek Park, and Sharon was still on her way.

My immediate greeters on the island were the familiar silver maples, in nearly full leaf, and the beech tree to the left of the bridge. The last time I saw the beech its buds were swelling, with silky hairs visible at their pointed tips where the tiny leaves and flowers were beginning to emerge. Today, the silkiness had disappeared from the leaves and flowers, and the leaves were already beyond their initial graceful downward swirl and holding themselves on a near-horizontal plane, where they will spend their lives as masters of photosynthesis. Their color: brilliant April lime green. The tiny male flowers, which dangle in round clusters, looked spent, like they'd released their pollen, and the female flowers transforming to fruit were adorably perky: tiny, round, and white, with erect curly pistils. I could already see their resemblance to the prickly brown husks formed last year and still attached to neighboring twigs.

On the right-hand side of the bridge, the basswoods that I last saw in tight, barely swelling winter bud less than two weeks ago were now bearing nearly full-sized heart-shaped leaves. As I was admiring the dangling, bell-like, purplish flowers in the adjacent pawpaw grove, Betsy rounded the bend from the statue plaza, dressed in pink running shorts with a small camel pack on her back. As she walked toward me, a black-and-white striped zebra swallowtail butterfly flew along beside her and then back to the pawpaw grove, from whence its caterpillar had earlier hatched from a tiny egg.

Sharon soon joined us, and the three of us admired the spring beauties, still shining bright, a few emerging Virginia waterleaf blooms, like small white fireworks, and delicate white umbels of sweet cicely flowers above fern-like leaves. When Jim and I were at the Ashby Inn we met Susan Leopold, the proprietor of the wonderful new Paris Apothecary at the inn, which her parents own. Susan is a PhD ethnobotanist who is partly descended from the Patawomeck Indians of Virginia. She and her daughters are members of the tribe. Susan wrote an amazing book that my eyes were instantly drawn to in her shop: *Isabella's Peppermint Flowers*, a children's book about finding the magic of spring beauties in the woods. I couldn't believe the serendipity. The day before, I had been showing the Smithsonian group the "candy-striped" flowers of spring beauty near the Joaquin Miller cabin at Milkhouse Ford in Rock Creek Park. Page five of Susan's book:

It wasn't really a patch of peppermint candy. But deep in the forest was a carpet of small white flowers with pink stripes that reminded the girls of peppermint candy. It was their favorite place. When the girls first discovered the patch of pink-and-white flowers, their mother had told them they were called *spring beauties*.[37]

This is a book not only filled with the childhood magic of forest discovery but also with educational information about taxonomy and botany specific to Virginia. As Susan notes, spring beauty's scientific name, *Claytonia virginica*, honors the botanist who contributed to *Flora Virginica*, which preceded today's *Flora of Virginia* by two centuries.

Sharon suggested that we head south on the trail, where we might get a glimpse of a brilliant yellow prothonotary warbler. The warbler eluded us, but we enjoyed a springtime stroll through the greening woodlands and wetlands, where arrow arum and other aquatic plants were unfurling. Occasional patches of golden ragwort, a spring-blooming member of the amazing daisy family with small yellow flower heads, blossomed near the shore. When we reached the inlet between TRI and Little Island, Sharon spotted four lesser scaup near the Virginia shore. Later, while watching a group of ring-billed gulls out on the water and a great blue heron fishing along the shore of Little

Island, two Caspian terns came winging into view above Little River, their red bills pointed riverward and their bodies all grace with pointed wings.

As we walked under the Roosevelt Bridge toward the Swamp Trail, Sharon and I talked about a whip-poor-will that Jim and I had heard outside our bedroom windows before dawn recently. A whip-poor-will hadn't been seen or heard in DC for many years, but, she said, a whip-poor-will has just been reported on the Rock Creek Park Golf Course. I was grateful for the official verification of what we heard, although the bird's voice had been thrillingly unmistakable.

We headed onto the boardwalk where the shining yellow flowers of swamp buttercup bloomed near the tidal inlet under greening willows bearing creamy flowering catkins. The white four-petaled flowers of spring cress appeared in discrete clumps along the boardwalk, their stalks about a foot tall. The little bamboo-like stalks of horsetail (*Equisetum*) bore thin feathery foliage.

Sharon was pressed for time so I didn't get a chance to check on the gnatcatcher nest near the bald-cypresses, as I wanted to keep up with her and see the birds that she would see. When we arrived at TR's plaza, we got a very good look at a hermit thrush, which will soon head north, possibly to Vermont where it sings so poignantly near my sister's rural home, or to the Adirondacks, where young Roosevelt enjoyed its song.

Those of us who love nature anxiously await the return of DC's official bird this time of year: the wood thrush. Both thrushes are consummate musicians. As I mentioned earlier in my island account, Roosevelt called the song of the hermit thrush "perhaps the sweetest music I have ever listened to," and he dubbed the wood thrushes at Sagamore Hill: "Our most beautiful singers..."[38] As we stood beneath the trees, Betsy recognized the song of the yellow-rumped warbler, which we saw fleetingly high up in the willow oaks surrounding the plaza.

Before leaving the island, we heard the iconic sound of the white-throated sparrow near the statue of the man who loved its song too. So soon to head north! Sharon had to hustle ahead up the Mount Vernon Trail, but Betsy and I lingered on the ramp with its view of Grandmother Sycamore. Betsy is taking pictures of Grandmother through the seasons.

As we admired the beloved tree, a large bird flew over the footbridge heading north up Little River. An osprey! My first osprey of the year at long last. Sharon and Betsy said they are nesting at the Washington Sailing Marina and in Kenilworth Aquatic Gardens, where I saw parents, nest, and nestlings last spring while leading a forest-bathing walk there. Perhaps they don't nest on the islands and are just very frequent visitors.

April 21st: Return of a Songster

On the evening of April 19th I was sitting under a tree on a wooded hill in Rock Creek Park above Pinehurst Branch prepping for a forest-bathing walk. Twilight was deepening under a thick cloud cover as I heard the flute-like song of a wood thrush, newly returned from the neotropics. I gazed into the greening canopy with a joyous heart as he sang his piercing flute-like song. I have to concur with Roosevelt when he called the wood thrushes "our most beautiful singers."[39]

As I write today, wild tropical rains and hail are battering the sunroom roof and—just now—the sun is shining. Where is the rainbow? I see only billowing white clouds racing off to the northeast in a suddenly blue sky.

Chapter Eleven

May—Fledglings

May 1st: Musings on Springtime Loss

Why does spring so often feel like the season of loss and of feeling lost? We have now lost Robert Frost's ephemeral gold and our world is green. This spring green will be as fleeting as the gold, giving way to the deeper greens of summer. Why do I feel so lost in its midst?

As I was mowing the lawn the other day with our old-fashioned rotary mower, I rounded a small patch of lily-of-the-valley plants. My heart rose as I looked forward to stooping down to inhale the fragrance of those delicate white bells with their power to evoke childhood memories. But as I got closer I realized that the flowers had already bloomed and were now dry and shrunken. While I was out leading nature walks hither and yon, the lilies of the valley in my own yard had bloomed, and I had missed them.

Is that what springtime loss is all about, that we can't keep up? I spend most of my days out of doors, leading walks and prepping to lead walks, nose to the flower, eye to the sky, feet touching earth. And yet still I feel that spring has sailed and I have missed the boat. At least that's the way I feel today despite having honored the ancient tradition of bathing my face in the May Day morning dew.

My feelings of loss and of being lost are compounded today by a feeling of helplessness. A blue jay pair has made a nest under the beach umbrella above the picnic table in our backyard. It is a sturdy-looking nest in a spot safe from predators. But will it be safe from the wind? Strong storms are forecast for later today, and while the female jay keeps her calm and steady vigil atop her eggs, and the male swoops in to feed her, I watch nervously from my dining-room "office," feeling powerless to protect the jay family from the increasingly capricious mid-Atlantic winds.

And what of all the other birds throughout the world who must now contend with weather that is more extreme and less predictable than ever? How often do we humans stop to think about their vulnerability to climate change?

The last two Saturdays have seen two huge marches in Washington and around the United States and the world. On April 22nd I took part in the March for Science on the Mall. As I stood in my cramped spot in the cold rain near the Washington Monument, I was surprised and warmed by a familiar voice from the podium: Betsy Lovejoy's dad, Tom, was one of the speakers, and, as she told me later, even she hadn't known he would speak. This past Saturday the People's Climate March brought hundreds of thousands to DC. I was prepping for a DC EcoWomen hike the next day and missed the Climate March, although I fell in love with one of the signs I saw in the press: "Ice Has No Agenda. It Just Melts." On the day of the march, DC tied its heat record for the date: 91 degrees (33C) on the second to last day of the month that would go down as the city's hottest April on record.

I have not made it over to the island since April 19th. Yet I have felt close to the Roosevelt legacy if not to the island itself over the past few days. I'm revisiting the pages of Candice Millard's *River of Doubt*. The former president, slowed by malaria and an injured leg, has just told his son Kermit that he will take a lethal dose of morphine so that the harrowing expedition along uncharted Amazonian waters can proceed without him, and Kermit has refused to let him. My reading flowed alongside preparation for the DC EcoWomen hike I led yesterday to Pulpit Rock, one of President Roosevelt's favorite places for rock scrambles in Rock Creek Park. On Saturday evening, as Climate Marchers were heading home in the unforgiving heat, I was lying back on the cool shaded surface of Pulpit Rock, my eyes looking up through the forest canopy toward a white sky, my ears serenaded by a wood thrush, my heart full of spring's ephemeral magic. For a time, I wasn't feeling lost at all. I hadn't reached Pulpit Rock by climbing up the face of it, like the ever-fearless adventurer TR, but I was having my own style of wild adventure, quiet and still.

May 5th: Jay Fate

Their fate is tied to mine. Soon after I wrote about the nesting jays on May Day, the stormy afternoon threatened their perch. As the beach umbrella began to collapse with the female jay underneath, I felt compelled to take some action. I rushed outside with duct tape, and I was able to tape the handle of the umbrella pole so tightly that I don't think it will come down unless a tornado comes through.

Meanwhile I have fallen in love with the pair of jays despite every attempt to remain detached and emotionally shielded from their uncertain near future. How very like us they are, with their home and their devotion! The jays are teaching me to take things one step at a time and to have faith.

I've been trying to understand the ways in which Roosevelt related to nature and how they compare to my own. Roosevelt was an opponent of cruelty to animals and a passionate conservationist of land and wildlife. He was also an enthusiastic hunter, a sport hunter as well as a hunter-naturalist, whose museum specimens are still on display in prominent natural history museums. As a young boy, he kept wild animals in his bedroom and also learned the craft of taxidermy, starting the "Roosevelt Museum of Natural History" in his home as an 8-year-old. I respect his fearless participation in the hunt, and his intimate knowledge of the creatures he engaged with in the wild as a naturalist and a hunter.

In his book *The Naturalist: Theodore Roosevelt, a Lifetime of Exploration, and the Triumph of American Natural History*, Smithsonian Supervisory Museum Specialist Darrin Lunde wrote:

Today, we all tend to limit our interactions with nature. We glimpse it through binoculars and telephoto lenses and rarely examine an animal in our hands or contend with its death as something that is perfectly natural. Theodore Roosevelt and those who built the field of museum naturalism did something few would dream of today: they had *visceral* experiences with nature. They collected animals for science and hunted them for sport, in the process developing a very intimate connection to the way nature really works.[40]

As a woman, a mother, and a vegetarian, I relate to nature in a very different way, feeling common ground with maternal devotion when I witness it outside the human world. Ingrained in me is the desire to protect. I share that desire with Roosevelt and yet it comes from a different personal well-spring. The most closely I have ever identified with wildlife was when, as a young breastfeeding mother, I watched another primate mother nursing her offspring at the National Zoo. I'll never forget that visceral jolt of recognition.

As I was taping up the pole with wind and rain whipping around us, "Mama Jay" let out a soft "tweedle tweedle," ending any hopes for my own detachment.

May 8th: Birthday of My Firstborn

Thirty-one years ago today I became a mother myself, and I have watched my daughter Sophie grow into an amazing and accomplished young woman. One of the things I like most about being human is the lifelong attachment we enjoy with our offspring.

Last evening (a Sunday), with wild gray clouds streaming across the sky and occasional fits of raindrops, Jim dropped me at the Virginia end of Key Bridge on his way to a business reception in Old Town Alexandria. We were both buoyed by good news from France: The moderate Emmanuel Macron had just defeated the right-wing xenophobic Marine Le Pen in the French presidential election.

"I hope this helps stem the global rush toward extreme nationalism represented by the 'Brexit' vote and our own election," I said to Jim as we absorbed the news.

Jim dropped me off at 5:30 p.m., and when I learned that the tide would be high at 6:51, I hoped to have a real shot at seeing it reverse in the tidal inlet. As I walked down the Mount Vernon Trail ramp, a few fluffy cottonwood seeds drifted across the paved path. Little River was high, wild, and brown, and I learned today that Great Falls was nearly at flood stage at the time, 25 feet above normal. In recent days I've led nature walks in Rock Creek Park, and tree tours at the Capitol, as well as a forest-bathing walk for 40 high-school freshmen on Sugarloaf Mountain. I've been out of touch with the river, and its high wild status was a surprise to me.

I stopped at the top of the ramp to look across Little River toward Grandmother, whose creamy white limbs were fully cloaked in her springtime leaves. A statuesque great blue heron stood on a boulder next to the leafing sycamore just above the racing brown waters. As I continued down the trail, the fragrances of Japanese honeysuckle and multiflora rose, two invasives that smell seductively sweet in bloom, mixed with the pleasing scent of fresh tar. Progress had been made on the refurbished stretch of the Mount Vernon Trail and on the parking lot, which must soon open to traffic again. Blackberries and tulip-trees were also blooming, the latter announcing their magnolia-family lineage with their beautiful tulip-like flowers, each yellow-green petal with an orange blush. A mystery rose-family tree at the entrance to the bridge was sporting small unripe apple-like fruit, too big to be crabapples and too long to be definitively apples. But they resembled apples more than anything else that came to mind. I bit into one of the fruits and it was bitter, with unripe seeds— displaying the genius of fleshy fruits, which are only delectable when the plant is ready for a passing animal to distribute the mature seeds.

I walked across the footbridge, which was haloed in swooping cliff swallows, lured on by the green island. The air felt fresh and clean, like New England mountain air, and I breathed deeply of it as I approached the familiar welcoming committee of silver maple, American elm, American beech, white mulberry, and basswood. I looked closely at the basswoods to see the tiny round flower buds dangling from the pale green leafy bracts near the ends of the branchlets. What a fragrance they will exude when they open! I imagined drinking the delicious, nourishing, and medicinal tea often brewed from closely related linden or lime (*Tilia*) flowers in Europe. European lindens are planted along many Washington streets and on the White House and Capitol grounds.

I decided to walk south along the island perimeter, and I soon ran into a smiling young man wearing binoculars and clutching a Sibley bird guide. He had just seen a great crested flycatcher and scarlet tanager in quick succession and had also spotted a yellow-rumped warbler and heard a parula warbler. Yesterday morning, I received an email from Betsy Lovejoy, who had seen 19 warbler species in Rock Creek Park the day before.

The pawpaw trees were putting forth a few shining new leaves, although most of their tropical-looking leaves were fully grown and settled into a duller mature green. The low-growing Virginia waterleaf plants still sported firework displays of white flowers. The trail was a rich chocolate brown color and the earth *smelled* like chocolate, while floral, fruity, and leafy smells emanated from the greening woods. An occasional silver maple leaf had landed, silvery side up, like a fragment of poetry, and I walked over many fallen tulip-tree petals. After watching so many ashes succumb to the emerald ash borer, I was pleased to see that the winged seeds or samaras lying in the path were of the white ash tree. I said a silent prayer for the survival and revival of the island's white and green ash trees.

I walked into the wetland near the shore on a fallen weathered tree, its bare inner bark bleached almost white. The scene was primordial. The shiny arrow-shaped leaves of arrow arum adorned the swampy terrain, and tall yellow irises bloomed. They are considered invasive, but I couldn't help admiring their yellow petals against the green of the verdant swampland. I saw a sedge that I thought might be *Carex intumescens* (later identified as *Carex grayi* by Rod Simmons, the botanist who visited the island with me during the winter and identified the plant after this walk based on one of my photographs and its tidal marsh habitat). Various nettle-family members were up, and the stinging nettle was beginning to bloom. The female spicebush plants were showing small green drupes.

This was my first walk on Theodore Roosevelt Island in high spring. As I sauntered along the chocolate trail, surrounded by the fragrant forest, I felt bathed in all that is fresh and new, in beauty born. Even the sounds of the occasional airplanes overhead were muffled by the rain-fed canopy. As I gazed into the lush crowns of the island trees, I thought of Roosevelt and how he savored the splendor of the Amazonian rainforest despite the perils of his journey, and how he also appreciated the beauty of our own local woods when he lived in Washington.

I left the island's dense western forest and rounded the bend to the southern end of the boardwalk, where I saw a redbud tree, its purply-pink flowers of early spring now morphed to green legumes dangling in the midst of heart-shaped leaves. The tidal inlet was high and brown, reflecting both high tide and the river nearing flood stage. As I stepped onto the boardwalk and into the open landscape of the marsh, the bright sharp "conkaree" of a red-winged blackbird sounded *dee*-lightful (as TR would say). I soon saw the bird near the top of a dead green ash in the midst of cattails, flexing his red wing-patches with each "conkaree." The shining yellow swamp buttercups were still blooming amid the feathery horsetails, and cottony seeds released from black willow catkins floated on the air.

As I approached the bald-cypress trees, with their new green needles, I heard the keening call of an osprey. I looked up to see two magnificent birds wheel into view above the inlet. My timing was perfect and not only because of the ospreys: High tide was 20 minutes away. I sat on the boardwalk between two bald-cypresses facing the inlet. I waited. The tide was still visibly incoming. I soon realized that 20 minutes was a long time to stare at the tide. I took the opportunity to turn around and search for the gnatcatcher nest. I was soon rewarded as I saw a gnatcatcher swoop in to the still-intact nest with food in her mouth for nestlings that were just out of sight.

The drama of the reversing tide was muted by the volume of water in the flooding river. The wind also caused a bit of confusion, but eventually I did see the flow of the water reverse. After a time it was clear that all the tulip-tree petals and willow and cottonwood seeds on the surface of the inlet had reversed course and were now headed riverward. Contemplating changing tides always comforts me in some deep way, perhaps because it reminds me, metaphorically, that the tides will always turn.

There were very few people on the island. I ran into the young birder again on the boardwalk, heading in the opposite direction. He told me he had seen a green heron near the outcrop I call Georgetown Rock and a black-crowned night heron on the Virginia shore. I never saw either bird, but when I reached Georgetown Rock, two great blue herons were standing near the shore in Zen-mode, and a Louisiana waterthrush was perched on a pile of sticks in the river, bobbing his or her tail. The bladdernuts nearby were loaded with dangling green lantern-like capsules.

It was growing dark as I headed back across the northern end of the island, and I had a long walk to the Rosslyn Metro station ahead of me. I picked up my pace but quickly slowed again when I came upon several clumps of lyre-leaved sage, a tallish mint-family member with small lilac-hued tubular flowers and basal rosettes of lyre-shaped leaves. It's always heartening to see native wildflowers thriving on the island in the midst of invasive plants.

When I reached the shore of Little River, I gazed into the crown of the tall cottonwood growing near Grandmother. High up in the tree, I could see segmented catkins that identified the tree as a female cottonwood, her fluffy seeds yet to be released. With admiration, I noted another companion of Grandmother: the neighboring tulip-tree that has been almost completely girdled by beavers. Astonishingly, it was in full leaf and flower, and the ground around it was speckled with petals.

I crossed the bridge in the gathering dusk and returned to the mainland with a full heart. Once home I found a favorite poem of a favorite poet in my inbox, sent by my Rock Creek walking buddy Carol Newman: "How I Go to the Woods" by Mary Oliver.

May 11th: Downriver to Mount Vernon

Today it is raining and the forecast calls for rain for the next three days. This morning the rain had already started when I went out to see how the nesting blue jays were faring. A nest is an island in the air and represents the same sort of tentative safety. Although her nest provides a separate terrain with a clear view of what lies beyond, it is vulnerable to external forces, the way I often feel these days.

Yesterday as I was driving down the George Washington Memorial Parkway toward Mount Vernon to do some research for a Smithsonian Associates lecture I'm giving later this month, I was drinking in the color green of the trees lining the road south of Old Town Alexandria. As I drove along the widening Potomac River south of Theodore Roosevelt Island, I marveled over the new leaves and their invisible tenacity. These tender-looking organs will remain on the trees from now through November, growing a deeper and duller green, in endless cycles of dust-gathering and rain-cleansing, surviving gale-force winds and likely drought and eventually changing color and falling to the earth for the next phase of their journey as components of the life-giving soil.

What a vulnerable-seeming piece of fabric is the leaf! Not even an eighth of an inch thick, easily crushed or torn, and hanging by a thread in all weathers and in the face of predatory insects and pathogens. And yet life on Earth depends on the thinner-than-a-wafer, light-as-a-feather green leaf for life and breath, food and oxygen.

How skewed is our human vision! When we think of power, we think of aggressive force, of conqueror and weaponry, of domination. And yet it is the thin green leaf that truly holds the power. Strip away too many of them and we are goners.

My heart leapt as I approached Mount Vernon, knowing that I had the whole afternoon to wander the acres where George Washington lived and nurtured his farm and his trees. I was happy to discover that three of the trees planted by Washington more than two centuries ago were still thriving. [2020 note: On March 2, 2018, the eastern hemlock planted circa 1791 came down in a severe storm with high winds.] I stationed myself at the foot of a tulip-tree that Washington planted in 1785, a tree I first visited as a 25-year-old researcher thrilled by the knowledge that George Washington loved trees. It was a perfect spring day, sunny and 70 degrees (21C). The tall tulip-tree was in full bloom, which I could see only with some serious neck-craning.

Gazing up along the tall trunk to the flowering and leafing crown, I took some pictures with my smartphone, hoping their quality would pass muster for my upcoming lecture (doubtful). As I was thus engaged, in the company of songbirds and a distant piccolo, a young family came down the path. For some reason, I felt compelled to let them know that this tree had been planted by George Washington.

The three children and their parents all broke into big grins and hurried over to touch the tree. When a petal landed on the trail, one of the two girls said, "Oh, these are the flowers we've been seeing!" They were from Seattle and had never seen a tulip-tree before their East Coast visit.

Caught up in their enthusiasm for the tree and its lavish orange, green, and yellow flowers, I said, "It's in the magnolia family."

In the ten minutes I spent in the company of this open-hearted family, I learned that they were traveling the country for a year, while the dad—Tim Shaffer—presented an assembly for schools titled "The Kindness Adventure." He told me that the presentations are based on his experiences in Kenya and incorporate a connection with Kenyan children, magic, and music, all to convey a message of kindness over bullying. His wife, Jen, and their three children have had quite an adventure traveling with their husband and dad. Tim has performed at the White House, interestingly not during the administration of our president of Kenyan descent, but during the George W. Bush administration.

We experienced instant rapport beneath George Washington's tree, and something compelled me to say: "We will survive like this tree." Like the vulnerable life-giving leaf, kindness is a powerful force.

I've noticed that references to our current president have taken on an indirect, unspoken quality as if we have already shielded ourselves from the worst toxins and are in a deeper place of long-term endurance. The name of the occupant of the Oval Office goes unspoken even on a day when the world has gone haywire over his firing of FBI Director James Comey and he has welcomed the Russian foreign minister and ambassador to the White House with no American journalists allowed in, only a photographer from TASS, the main Russian news agency.

After communing with the trees planted by George Washington (another tulip-tree and a hemlock, plus a flowering buckeye dating nearly to his time), I walked over to the black locust grove north of the mansion that still grows in the spot where General Washington directed his grounds manager to plant it from New York in 1776. A blue Atlas cedar from the Atlas Mountains of northern Africa beckoned from its perch overlooking the Potomac, where it was planted in 1874. I walked across the grass to the tree and sat down in a soft bed of needles, under its spreading branches with their bluish foliage. It was a cool spot for a warm day, with the view that inspired Washington below me—the river wide after its short journey from the fall zone in Washington, capital site chosen by the former owner of this very property.

After a respite under the Atlas cedar, I walked to the gravesite of George and Martha Washington. There, a related tree, a cedar of Lebanon—planted by a delegation of Masons in 1899 on the centennial of Washington's death—stands sentinel. Its upper branches held giant upright barrel-shaped cones.

There have been numerous improvements at Mount Vernon since my last visit, including the recreation of a home for enslaved people, representing the dark and oft overlooked side of Mount Vernon history. I was glad to see a reminder of the grim reality of slavery, even as I told myself that Washington freed enslaved people at Mount Vernon upon his death. However, I couldn't shake away the historic and contemporary darkness during dinner later at the Mount Vernon restaurant. I reminded myself of the young family I had met and their message of intercontinental kindness. I remembered the exuberance of children of all races who'd fanned out across the Mount Vernon grounds during my visit, more attuned to their own dramas and freedom from the classroom than the history of the place. I hope they will have plenty of time to ponder—and make—history during their long lives.

On the way home, I stopped at River Farm, which was owned by George Washington, to take pictures of a 200-year-old osage-orange in the "garden calm" and to check on the black walnut in the field near the river that probably dates to Washington's time. Heading north, I drove through a snowy flurry of cottonwood seeds as I passed Theodore Roosevelt Island, still surrounded by a brown river, high and wild.

May 30th: Fledge!

Our backyard avian adventure had the happiest ending—at least to the point where this wingless creature is able to follow the plot. Three jay nestlings—who were scrawny and panting in the heat just a few days ago—fledged early Sunday morning while Jim and I were still slumbering and dreaming.

Both jay parents were nearby on Saturday, flying in but not feeding their newly plumped and fluffed babes. When the adults came near, all the nestlings flapped their little wings. I watched as one of the parents attacked a nearby squirrel. As the squirrel responded by diving into a flowerpot, I felt I was in the midst of a Beatrix Potter tale.

I should have known that the squirrel attack was a clue that the parents were preparing for the big event. I woke up early Sunday morning and immediately came down to check the nest. Empty. Those jays were gone. Jim and I saw glimpses of adult jays off and on throughout the day, but the fledglings had disappeared, into the depths of the Leyland cypresses, up into the oak trees, or off down the block.

When we inspected the nest we were awed. Largely built by the female, with materials gathered by the male (some rejected twigs still lying on the picnic table weeks later), it was a *tour de force* of weaving: twigs, heavy-duty plastic fasteners and ties, the natural and the plastic all woven together with symmetrical artistry, with softer more flexible materials lining the center. After the jays fledged we read everything we could about their species. According to the sources we found online, including the Cornell ornithology website, the family will stay together for several weeks and the parents possibly for life. Jays are in the Corvid family, along with crows, magpies, and ravens; intelligent, sociable birds all.

In the world of humans, the immediate political front is a disaster. After Trump fired the FBI director, he shared classified information with the Russian ambassador and foreign minister, and now a special prosecutor has been appointed to look into possibly criminal ties between Russians and his campaign. Today it's a mighty challenge to focus on the power of the good, and without my connection to nature I don't know where I'd be emotionally.

My three Smithsonian Associates events are now behind me—a "City of Trees" lecture and book-signing, and two tree-tours of the Capitol grounds last week, one through the rain. I gave each event my all, and I will do so again for my events this week, starting with a forest-bathing walk for the Audubon Naturalist Society tomorrow in Rock Creek Park. The day after my Mount Vernon trip, I visited President Lincoln's Cottage to check on some of the historic trees that I like to feature in my lectures: another ancient osage-orange, a basswood, and a female ginkgo. Abraham Lincoln and his family lived at the cottage, several miles from the White House, in what was then called the Soldiers' Home during the summers he was president, and he commuted back and forth on horseback and by carriage, sometimes at great peril, during the height of the Civil War. After checking to see that all trees were thriving, I headed into the gift shop to find a knowledgeable person to answer some questions. An hour and a half later, Jamie Cooper, himself a member of the North Carolina Lumbee tribe, had enlightened me about the expanded mission of Lincoln's Cottage.

No longer simply a historic association designed to protect the legacy of the Lincolns living at the cottage, President Lincoln's Cottage, a non-profit organization now independent of the Trust for Historic Preservation that was responsible for the initial renovation a few years ago, is working to combat modern-day slavery and human trafficking here in DC and around the world. Each year in June since 2013 they have brought teenagers here from around the world to learn how to recognize and fight trafficking in their countries and to become part of a global network called "Students Opposed to Slavery" or SOS. President Lincoln's Cottage is also working to help and support immigrants. Jamie told me that Lincoln was very concerned with the treatment and integration of immigrants. In these two arenas—slavery and immigration—they are keeping Lincoln's legacy alive.

Just as I felt at Mount Vernon, after meeting the "Kindness Adventure" family at George Washington's tree, I came away from Lincoln's Cottage feeling inspired and full-hearted. Led by my love of trees, my world expanded.

٭

Chapter Twelve

June—Island Forest Bathing

June 3rd: June Comes to the Island

Donald Trump has moved to pull the USA out of the Paris Climate Agreement, which has been signed by 195 countries. Trump is aggressively moving in opposition to almost every policy I care about. While he and right-wing Republicans do everything they can to pull back women's reproductive rights, shutting down access to safe legal abortions and trying to roll back coverage for birth control, there's also a move to limit food aid to poor families with more than six members.

The news is disheartening as our lives go on. This morning I met Sadie, her husband Steve Hay, and friend Sieren Ernst, Gabe Popkin and his girlfriend Elana Goldstein, and Betsy Lovejoy and Tim Reed (Kingfisher Court members) at the bridge to the island. Ospreys flew overhead and dove for fish. Cliff swallows swooped under the bridge as Sadie, Betsy, and I climbed down to the Virginia shore to see them flying in and out of their nests.

We'll have to paddle under the bridge to glimpse the nestlings.

We took our time crossing the footbridge, so engaging were the birds. In an embarrassment of avian riches, bald eagles, a red-tailed hawk, and a pileated woodpecker joined the ospreys in the sky, a juvenile great blue heron fished along the Virginia shoreline, and two improbably vivid male wood ducks paddled down Little River. It was like a big bird zoo! Once we were on the island, we saw a Baltimore oriole and an indigo bunting, both of them showing off their arresting colors — one orange and black and the other indigo — from the crowns of dead ash trees.

Turtles of all sizes basked on riverside logs, and we spotted two five-lined skinks (small lizards) and several yellow-and-black spiders who had crafted impressive webs across large hollow stumps.

The trees were showing off too, the basswoods with yellow-green flower buds attached to pale green leafy bracts, a few of the buds opening, the beeches loaded with prickly golden husks, and the cottonwoods delivering flying cotton to the skies. The whitened limbs of Grandmother and her kin disappeared into lushly leafed crowns.

When we arrived at Georgetown Rock, Tim noticed a few shrubs with pink flowers way out on the farthest rocks. The tide was low, and he and I were able to climb out over the slippery slimy rocks to where they were growing. How thrilled I was to discover that they were native swamp roses, with small curved prickles, and flowers exuding the old-fashioned fragrance of a real rose! Tim was totally charmed. He and Betsy are a wonderful couple who share a deep love of nature and outdoor athleticism. They run and bike everywhere they go. It was gratifying to see him so impacted by the beauty of the island.

I found a sugar maple growing near Georgetown Rock, and then Gabe, a talented and prominent young science writer with an eye for trees, found a nearby Norway so we could compare features. People often confuse the two, but when you have them side by side the differences in leaves, buds, and bark are diagnostic. I suggested we give the trees the "Canadian flag test."

"Does the leaf look like the leaf on the Canadian flag?" I asked. "If it does, it's a sugar."

We also examined the mustard-colored newly emerging buds of a young bitternut hickory, and then admired the unofficial DC champion.

Then off we went down the boardwalk and into the swamp. The tiny umbels of honewort were blooming above three-parted leaves. Honewort is also called wild chervil and has a delightful flavor, like celery. Both plants are in the carrot or parsley family, a plant family requiring special foraging vigilance due to its mix of edibles and poisons. We nibbled the tasty leaves as we walked. When we found a silky dogwood blooming, I pulled out my hand lenses so we could get a close-up view of the little four-parted star-shaped flowers. With ten-times magnification, we could see multitudes of ants parading across the flower clusters.

The bald-cypress needles were a brilliant green, and stalkless fragrant cones were forming on the trees. Narrow-leaved cattails were blooming, the flowers borne in interrupted clusters, with males at the top and females below. If you run your hands over them the males release clouds of yellow pollen, while the females feel like silk or satin.

When we reached the southern end of the Swamp Trail, a female mallard and six fuzzy yellow ducklings were paddling across the inlet between TRI and Little Island, and a pair of Canada geese with three goslings were swimming in the opposite direction. Our small flock of nature lovers headed back through the chocolate-scented woods and across the Little River footbridge, returning to our to-do lists and the news of the day with nature-nourished hearts.

June 14th: New York Nature and the Fledged Jays

Last weekend during my visit to New York my son Jesse and I watched the full strawberry moon rise over Washington Square Park, a small green island in an urban sea. We celebrated the natural world in the midst of that great city by exploring the archipelago of nature that exists even there—walking the High Line and visiting the Conservatory Garden in the northern part of Central Park.

When Jesse was born 26 years ago today and we returned home with him to Strawberry Moon Farm in Comus, the crescent strawberry moon was low on the western horizon next to a rare alignment of planets: Venus, Jupiter, and Mars. I always associate Jesse's birth with the magic of nature: the planets, the farm, and the honeysuckle my nature-loving friend Liz Wedam brought me just before he was born.

The fireflies will light up this place in a few hours. I'm sitting at the picnic table in the backyard, which is our domain again now that the jays have fledged. There is a deep powder-blue hydrangea in full bloom tucked in between the garden fence and the southern side of the house near the picnic table. Blue hydrangeas are Nantucket flowers, island of my first love. This morning I woke to more news of violence: A shooter took aim at a baseball practice in a park in Alexandria. Congressional Republicans were practicing for a traditional game against Democrats scheduled for tomorrow in Nationals Park. No one was immediately killed except the shooter, but there were several serious injuries, including a pelvic injury to House Majority Whip Steve Scalise of Louisiana who is in critical condition. I have just learned that another shooting occurred today at a UPS facility in San Francisco, where four people are dead, including the gunman.

The Capitol Police who comprised Scalise's protection detail acted quickly and prevented further injury in Alexandria. I try to remember that they are always poised for action. In my interactions with them on the Capitol grounds they seem so relaxed and friendly, despite being visibly armed to the teeth. Yesterday I had a pleasant chat with an officer near the western front of the Capitol as I consulted with him about logistics for an upcoming bike trip I'm leading for Casey Trees. We'll begin at REI's flagship store, the former Coliseum, site of the first live Beatles concert in the USA, and bike to the Capitol, where I'll lead a tree tour on the grounds.

Whither the Island, refuge during times of ongoing national travail? A week ago today I led a *shinrin-yoku* or "forest bathing" walk there, sponsored by the Audubon Naturalist Society. The day was cool and overcast, with occasional showers in the forecast. The showers never materialized, and our small group— all women as the one male registrant didn't show—enjoyed the cool morning, especially with the knowledge that serious heat was on the way.

When I arrived in the parking lot, Alyssa Pease, a landscaper who has been on many of my Rock Creek Park walks, was standing under a tall sycamore next to Little River, smilingly gazing into the branches of a musclewood tree. She exuded the sense of serenity that I hoped people would attain during the walk. There was much I wanted to impart about the practice of forest bathing, the history of the island, and Roosevelt, the naturalist, as we stood on the footbridge above Little River. And yet I wanted to exude calmness and serenity.

I began by describing the practice of *shinrin-yoku*, instigated by the Japanese Forestry Agency in the 1980s with roots in ancient Shinto and Buddhist nature traditions. In Japan there are now several dozen forests designated for forest bathing, and millions of Japanese people relieve urban stress and long work-hours by visiting these forests and soaking up the beauty of nature through all their senses. Extensive studies before and after *shinrin-yoku* walks have demonstrated their benefits, showing lowered cortisol levels and lowered blood pressure.

Health studies in Japan, in South Korea, where the practice of forest bathing is called *sanlimyok*, in Europe, and in North America have also shown increased immunity to disease and improved mood and cognition.

Amos Clifford, who founded the Association of Nature and Forest Therapy Guides and Programs in California five years ago, adapted the practice for North Americans and, working with his partner Sky Maria Buitenhuis, has now expanded its reach to include forest-therapy guide trainings around the world.

I imparted a bit of health data and my own forest-bathing story, and then talked about what a fitting memorial the wild island is to Theodore Roosevelt, the naturalist. With Little River flowing beneath the bridge, Grandmother and her friends beckoning from the island shore, and the White House just a short crow's flight away, I read the following passage from Darrin Lunde's book, *The Naturalist*:

"Even from the presidential residence, Theodore Roosevelt found ways to engage with his beloved nature. The White House, with its patchwork of trees, shrubs, and open lawns, was a perfect songbird habitat...Roosevelt sometimes paid more attention to the birds perched outside the White House windows than to the statesmen seated inside. One morning he burst into a Cabinet meeting with startling news. 'Gentlemen, do you know what has happened this morning?' he squawked. Every man in the room feared national crisis, but, to their surprise, the president chirped, 'I just saw a chestnut-sided warbler—and this only in February!'"[41]

I then quoted from the large stone "Nature" tablet behind the plaza where we would have maple-sap tea at the close of our walk: "There are no words that can tell the hidden spirit of the wilderness, that can reveal its mystery, its melancholy and its charm."[42]

We all introduced ourselves and talked about our love of nature. I gave my "embrace the human sounds of the traffic and planes" pep talk as the planes screeched overhead.

We walked quietly across the bridge and were greeted on the island shore by breezes stirring up the silvery undersides of the silver maple leaves. On one side of the footbridge, an American beech was abundantly adorned with prickly golden fruit husks, and on the other, the American basswoods were beginning to open their small, fragrant yellow flowers.

As we walked toward the tall Shumard oak near the northwestern shore, we passed beneath a thick canopy of tropical-looking pawpaw leaves. Alyssa spotted a small cluster of pawpaw fruits, and we all gazed appreciatively and aspiringly up at them. Someone noted that they wouldn't ripen until fall; and another that we didn't have a prayer of beating the island's residents to those tasty fruits, in flavor and texture a cross between a mango and a banana.

I had loaned each participant a portable fabric tripod stool and I invited them to set them up in a circle beneath the bountiful crown of the Shumard oak. Noting that he had spent three nights camping with President Roosevelt in Yosemite, I quoted from that passionate forest wanderer and protector, John Muir: "Another glorious day, the air as delicious to the lungs as nectar to the tongue."[43] After sharing Muir's words, I asked people to "breathe deeply and feel the way our breath connects us to the life of the forest."

After a few minutes of silence, during which birds sang and breezes stirred, we packed up our tripod stools, and I gave the next invitation: "As we walk, notice what's in motion." We walked north, past Grandmother and her riverside bedrock home, to the concrete slab that marks the site of the old causeway to Virginia.

Here I invited people to celebrate their connection to the river, noting, just as I had the previous summer before a Casey Trees kayaking trip: "We are made up of 60 to 70 percent water, and therefore the Potomac River, source of Washington's drinking water, is quite literally our life's blood."

As fluffy white cottonwood seeds swirled around us, some of us walked north and some south. Before heading back toward Grandmother, I noticed that Clare Kelley, who just completed her own forest-therapy guide training, had taken off her shoes and was stepping into the river.

I found Grandmother and her far-reaching network of multi-hued roots. Standing under her and facing Little River, I fixed my gaze on the Virginia shoreline. After a few minutes I decided to take off my shoes and immerse my feet in the river, something I wouldn't have done back in the 1960s. Grandmother has known the river through all her twentieth- and twenty-first-century stages of health.

Perching myself on one of Grandmother's stalwart horizontal roots, I dipped my bare feet in the river. This felt wonderful. My feet bobbed a little with the flowing river and outgoing tide. The liquid embrace of Little River, and the gently rustling leaves of Grandmother's crown, lulled me into such a relaxed state that I forgot I was the one to keep the time. I put on my shoes and socks and raced back to the causeway.

Clare returned to the causeway from her river experience not only with wet feet but also with purple fingers, stained with mulberry juice. She invited us to taste the delicious fruits ready to pluck from the branches overhanging Little River. The white mulberry was brought here from Asia with the goal of establishing a silk industry, boosted by the interests of President John Quincy Adams and other early leaders. The tree has become invasive throughout the Washington region, but invasive plants are not without their attributes. Wineberries, abundant on the island and soon to ripen, also come to mind.

After our mulberry feast, we set up our stools next to Little River, and we shared our solo experiences with the river. It had inspired deep relaxation and appreciation in all of us.

Clare said: "The sense that this mighty river is flowing through me gives me a close, personal connection to it."

We then headed across the northern tip of the island toward Georgetown Rock, and I invited everyone to open all their senses and to be aware of the way the ground feels beneath your feet when you're walking, adding: "The pebbled path we'll be walking on is the old route between the causeway to Virginia and the Mason ferry to Georgetown, and may date as far back as the eighteenth century."

We set up our stools in a circle amid the rocks and roots near Georgetown Rock. Here I invited everyone to contemplate the word "treasure" as both a noun and a verb. I told them I sometimes think of Theodore Roosevelt Island as Treasure Island, especially in the vicinity of Georgetown Rock. I then asked them to spend a few minutes searching for treasure or for something *to* treasure.

One participant found a cluster of pawpaw seeds, and she made a small work of art with the seeds and a piece of bark lying on the ground and other found natural materials. Another found unripe wild grapes to treasure visually. I had walked out toward Georgetown Rock, although the tide was too high to climb onto the rock outcrop as I had done with Tim a few days earlier. After everyone else had shared their treasures, either verbally or visually, I invited them to come see the wild native roses growing on the rock and also to smell the flowers on a low-hanging bough of a basswood tree nearby—"my" treasures.

We then headed toward the interior of the island. I showed them some light green bladdernut capsules and we opened one to find a shiny green seed inside; "like a pearl in an oyster," someone said. We visited the large bitternut hickory near the entrance to the swamp. Walking back toward the statue and plaza, we heard and saw an indigo bunting singing from the top of a dead ash tree. Spicebush grew along the trail, and I invited everyone to scratch and sniff a fragrant spicy twig. We also crushed one shiny little green spicebush drupe, releasing its fragrance into the air, astonishingly like a classic spicy aftershave.

"These little drupes will ripen to red, fueling wood thrush journeys of more than a thousand miles," I told the group.

When I mentioned that spicebush was in the same delicious plant family as our native sassafras, cinnamon, bay, laurel, and avocado, the news resonated with everyone; they had all caught hints of cinnamon and bay in the smell of the twig.

Alyssa smiled and said, "Those leaves look like the leaves of an avocado plant."

We also found a green husk containing a hard nut on the ground, and I urged everyone to smell that too. It exuded a spicy buttery smell that a friend once said "smells like key lime pie." Most people were surprised to learn that the nut inside this rich citrusy package was a black walnut.

We entered the plaza from the southeastern side and walked under the circle of willow oaks, up the steps and over the moat, and across the large stone plaza with TR to our right, his arm upstretched, to the northwestern side of the plaza, where I began setting up our closing "tea." As I spread a blue and green Indian cloth on the stone at the top of the northwestern steps, I noticed that most of the group had gravitated to the nearby "Nature" tablet, where they were quietly reading Roosevelt's words—words that I had shared as we began our journey over the footbridge. Dry willow oak leaves and white ash samaras adorned the stone around me.

Everyone eventually climbed the steps to join me, and I asked Clare to give the last invitation, which she did with heartfelt eloquence: communion with a tree. As everyone else dispersed to find a tree to sit or stand under for a few last quiet moments, I unpacked my Japanese teacups, pure maple sap, maple candies, and walnuts. I gave everyone a few more minutes to commune with their chosen tree, and then I called them back to where I had poured sap into the teacups and set out the maple candies and walnuts.

As we drank our tea, and passed around and savored the candies and walnuts, I asked for volunteers to read the two poems with which I close every forest-bathing walk: Mary Oliver's "Wild Geese" and Wendell Berry's "The Peace of Wild Things." I never have to wait more than a few seconds for someone to volunteer to read those widely beloved poems.

I then shared a couple of quotes from TR's friend and colleague John Muir: "In every walk with nature one receives far more than he seeks,"[44] and "I only went out for a walk, and finally concluded to stay out till sundown, for going out, I found, was really going in."[45]

I asked people to share something they would bring back to the world with them from this experience. Along with specific experiences they said they would remember—the smell of a spicebush twig, the taste of mulberries, the flow of the wide river—each person in turn expressed a profound need for quiet time spent in nature in a world that seems to grow crazier and less certain by the day.

June 27th: A Glorious Day

"Another glorious day, the air as delicious to the lungs as nectar to the tongue!" Just before sitting down to write, I saw two adult-looking jays visit the bird feeder. They *looked* like adults, but the one perched at the top of the feeder seemed a little wobbly, and when the one lower on the feeder flew up and seemed to feed the one at the top, my heart sang.

The thermometer dipped into the 50s (10–15C) last night, a June miracle in Washington. Today the sun is shining from a blue sky, and the cool air holds no trace of humidity. The hydrangeas near the garden fence reflect the blue of the sky and all is lush around me, with song sparrows singing from the canopy. Yesterday a friend emailed a recording of Bryn Terfel singing "June Is Bustin' Out All Over," a song from the classic musical *Carousel* that I mentioned last summer. I had forgotten that Virginia creepers, native vines of Theodore Roosevelt Island, are mentioned in the song and in exuberant fashion.

I may have stepped foot on the island for the last time during my year of record. The island is now closed for several weeks for removal of the green and white ashes that are victims of the emerald ash borer. The dead and brittle trees are considered a hazard for island visitors. I'm leading three paddling trips in upcoming days—one for the Friends of Theodore Roosevelt Island, one for the Audubon Naturalist Society, and one for a group of friends. I will be able to view the island from close to the shore, but I won't be able to walk upon it.

I worry about the effects on birds and other wildlife and plants during this tree removal, and I certainly hope it's sensitively done. I expressed concern to the Friends of Theodore Roosevelt Island and had a long conversation with a friend who is an ecologist. I have concluded, perhaps in a rather cowardly way, that any further action is out of my hands and I have to trust the National Park Service. I know there will be trauma, but I hope that nesting birds will have fledged by the time the trees are removed.

My last visit to the island was sweet. I had just finished leading a bicycling tree tour for Casey Trees on a beautiful day. We biked from REI to the Capitol, where I led a 1½-hour tree tour. The one sad note in an otherwise joyful event was the sight of the largest tree on the Capitol grounds, a willow oak, lying on the ground and cut in segments, having fallen victim to a storm the previous Monday. I have always concluded my tree tours of the Capitol with a visit to that incredible oak, sharing the news that willow oaks were favorite trees of Thomas Jefferson. Given the current political climate, I couldn't help but feel this loss symbolically. I imagined how Thomas Jefferson would feel to see the tree lying on the ground. The old giant was felled by wind, not directly by human hands, but Jefferson's words echoed in my mind: "The unnecessary felling of a tree, perhaps the growth of centuries, seems to me a crime little short of murder; it pains me to an unspeakable degree."[46] Many of our historic trees are falling victim to stormy winds amped up by climate change, perhaps including this old and beloved oak on the Capitol grounds.

After the tour, I cycled over to Jim's office and we popped my bike in the back of his truck for the drive to Theodore Roosevelt Island. When we arrived, Little River was filled with colorful kayaks and canoes. As we waited for a parking spot, we watched an orange-and-black monarch butterfly, the first we've seen this year, nectaring in a tall fragrant cluster of dusky-pink milkweed flowers. Once on foot and approaching the island bridge, I asked Jim to weigh in on the mystery tree to the left of the bridge that has stumped many botanists. I had concluded from the flowers and fruit that it is some unusual type of apple tree, but the still-small green fruits are sort of oblong and I'm the most cautious botanist, reluctant to jump to conclusions.

Jim said, "Yes, of course those are apples," and to prove his point he picked one and took a bite, not even flinching at the bitter taste of the unripe fruit. "That's an apple," he stated, digging through the remaining flesh to show me the seeds in their papery chambers.

After Jim's definitive apple identification, we crossed the bridge, where families with children of all ages, babies in strollers, and dogs of every shape and size—including a corgi pup—were coming and going. Cliff swallows, short of tail (for swallows) and pale of rump, were swooping and diving all around the bridge above Little River. The island beckoned with its alluring lushness and the verdant fragrance of young summer. The dead green ashes were as enfolded into the healthy canopy and as visually muted as the blighted cherry-blossom buds had been among the thriving blossoms at the Tidal Basin in March. June was "bustin' out all over," and the air was "delicious to the lungs."

We walked under the tropical-looking pawpaw grove to the Shumard oak, where I showed Jim that a path off to the right led up to the plaza. "Let's take it," he said. So off we went through the fragrant spicebush, the tall wingstem plants, and an ocean of white avens in bloom, and up to the plaza, where we listened to the fountains and read every quote on every tall stone tablet. Along the way, a large dark dragonfly alit on a wingstem plant, and a rain of mystery seeds fell on our heads from the tall trees.

We then headed over to Georgetown Rock, frequently dining on trailside wineberries, newly ripe. I always tell people, "It's our duty to eat the wineberries so that birds won't spread the seeds of this invasive plant." Friends of Theodore Roosevelt Island are diligently working to remove wineberry plants, but in the meantime, one must eat.

Chapter Thirteen

July—Paddling to Shore

July 1st: A Journey in the Heat

And so begins the month that brings me full circle to the tandem flight of the kingfisher. It is a classic Washington summer day, the temperature 90 degrees (32C) with a chance of thunderstorms later this afternoon. After trying to read the tea leaves in the sky, I just gave the basil, tomatoes, and green peppers in the backyard a soaking with the hose.

Our series of cool clear June days, during which I was dancing with joy on my bare toes, is well behind us and summer is really here. The balmy weather blessed us during a week when I was leading no field trips and I was giddy with freedom from constant prep. I went to Norman's Farm Market and lingered over the white and yellow peaches, blackberries, tomatoes, squashes, and corn. I made dinners for Jim and me with the fresh fruits and vegetables. I cleaned my office, and caught up on long-overdue correspondence. I got together with friends. I'm at the age where many of my friends are retiring, and although I have no desire to do so myself, I felt the lure last week during my bout of leisure.

Wow, the rains have come and it's a deluge! Our poor basil must be drowning. The temperature has dropped 17 degrees with the rain! I just stepped out on the front porch where the air is drunk and fragrant with herbs: lavender, fennel, basil, rosemary, oregano, and thyme.

Yesterday, with the thermometer topping out at 93 degrees (99-degree heat index or 37C), I went on a rather ambitious adventure, although I doubt that Roosevelt, champion of the strenuous life, would have been impressed. I rode my bike to the Georgetown waterfront, hopped in a kayak, and paddled from the Key Bridge boathouse all the way around Theodore Roosevelt Island in a gusty southern breeze, and then rode the 7½ miles uphill during the hottest part of the day.

The ride to the river on the Capital Crescent Trail—an old rail route—is thrilling. It's a downhill joy-ride under shady trees for much of the way. You sail down the hill near Little Falls, cross the C&O Canal and towpath, and then pass Fletcher's Cove. Just before the cove, wineberries line the trail, and they were ripe and ready for the plucking yesterday. The most accessible fruits had all been taken, but it felt worth it to risk picking up ticks by going a little deeper into the bush.

About a mile or so past the cove there's a break in the tree canopy, offering up a stunning river panorama. A couple of dead trees there held cormorants, who were perched stoically on the bare branches like so many black-robed monks. After the cormorant trees, I began to see glimpses of Key Bridge and the river's bevy of white and colored boats, and then, suddenly, I was in Georgetown.

I slipped into a green kayak, two bottles of water at my feet, my pack strapped into the prow, and off I went under the second arch of Key Bridge as the first was under construction. From the get-go it was not easy paddling and it got harder as the afternoon wore on. The wind was out of the south, which made the trip down to the island and along the western shore difficult, and the trip back did not feel like the "wind at your back" scenario I had anticipated during the first half of my journey. Remembering the Casey Trees trip last summer, when we all sailed along on our way downriver on a northwest breeze, barely lifting a paddle and struggling to linger at the trees, I imagined the same would be true for me on my return trip. However, as I learned from the Fletcher's Boathouse manager (when I stopped for crackers and a power drink on my bike ride home), the southern wind is more fickle than the northern.

Despite the challenging kayaking, I thoroughly enjoyed my nature adventure on the river. I paddled under the trees that are now old friends: silver maples, sycamores, river birches, cottonwoods, American elms, and black walnuts. I came in close to shore to admire a cluster of fringed loosestrife, with its nodding yellow star-like flowers, next to the remains of the old causeway. The pickerelweed was in full bloom, its flower clusters like so many purple candles rising above shiny heart-shaped leaves. A large dark dragonfly flew alongside my kayak.

When I paddled under Grandmother's bountiful limbs, I encountered a heart-warming sight. Little River was rising, less than two hours from highest tide, and most river rocks near Grandmother were submerged. On the two protruding ones, I saw a female mallard and her brood of five. On rock one, two fluffy yellow babes were scrunched under her belly next to her bright orange legs, and on rock two, three fluffy ducklings were snuggled together and snoozing. I lingered for a long time near Grandmother. After a time, the six of them launched themselves into the river, the five ducklings paddling manically about while Mama Mallard quacked an insistent warning not to go too far afield. I would never have the maternal nerves required to keep track of wayward ducklings.

While paddling past Grandmother I assessed the nearness to

her of several dead ashes and got a pain in my gut trying to imagine how the tree-removal crew is going to take down the dead trees without damaging the other trees of the forest.

On a brighter note, other summer wildflowers were coming along. The lizard's tail was in full bloom, each white-flowering spike like an upright tail. It bloomed near large clusters of arrow arum (past bloom), and spatterdock (still to come). The pale lavender-pink flowers of the American germander or wood sage, square-stemmed member of the mint family, had begun to appear. The trumpet creeper was in raging red bloom, but I searched the vines in vain for hummingbird visitors. The Virginia creeper was also blooming, although far less showily. I saw no cliff swallows circling the footbridge, and I think I've lost my chance to see nestlings from a paddling position. When I reached the inlet between Theodore Roosevelt Island and Little Island, two large birds stood sentinel high up in dead ash trees: a great blue heron and an osprey. The osprey flew downriver toward Memorial Bridge and landed in a dead ash on Little Island. The bird flew and landed again, and with each flight I got to admire his or her white breast and rusty-brown back feathers. Together we traveled around Little Island.

Turtles were basking on every available river log and snag. One old geezer had a front leg raised, and I immediately thought of the statue of TR with uplifted arm. Another turtle was perched on a snag far out in the middle of the Georgetown Channel, dramatically posed in front of the Kennedy Center like a distinguished patron of the arts.

I saw basswoods with heart-shaped leaves and small dry round fruits hanging from their leafy bracts (the "bats and balls"), and a few still-living green ashes or parts of green ashes bearing lavish clusters of samaras. It was highest tide when I got to Georgetown Rock, and I was able to paddle all the way around the rock that I walked to with Tim a few weeks ago. The swamp rose shrubs were covered with reddish rose hips, but a few pink flowers still bloomed. I tried but failed to kayak close enough to smell that sweet wild-rose fragrance. On the other side of Georgetown Rock, a ninebark plant was loaded with little clusters of follicles and leaves like small red maple leaves but arranged alternately. A smooth alder plant also clung to the rock.

As I was engaged in botanical wonderings, another female mallard with seven tiny ducklings came paddling around the rock in the company of a larger flock of mallards of all ages and stages.

I paddled hard back to the Key Bridge arches and the boathouse dock, wondering why that wind didn't feel as though it was at my back. I had a long hot uphill ride ahead of me, but my heart was full and so was my camel pack, although the ice I'd added hours before was long since melted. I paced myself and stopped at Fletcher's Cove for that sustenance, making it all the way back home none the worse for wear after six hours of exercise in the 90-plus-degrees heat (over 32C).

And that longing for adventure that I've been experiencing? Looks like I'm going to the North Dakota badlands in September to speak at a symposium about Roosevelt the naturalist, and then to Japan in October to visit the *shinrin-yoku* forests and health researchers that I've been reading about for the past few years.

July 3rd: Whither the Republic?

First of all, some good news here at home. The patience of a mourning dove (or as Sadie's young nephew says: "good morning dove") nesting on Sophie's former bedroom windowsill has paid off. I thought the dove was sitting in vain, day after day, but after many days of quiet vigilance, there is a big fluffy gray dovelet sitting in the haphazard-looking nest. And some quick research tells me that my assumption that the patient parent atop the single egg was always the female must be amended, as both mourning dove parents incubate their eggs and take turns feeding their young from a crop.

Dove news aside, I am feeling extremely disheartened on this Independence Day Eve. Is this what the founders risked everything for? So that a petty vindictive individual could peck out spiteful misogynistic tweets from the White House? Vicious tweets insulting yet another female journalist, Mika Brzezinski. Reporter Megyn Kelly drew his ire during the campaign. In both cases he used bloody images to insult and demean these extremely accomplished journalists. He also tweeted a doctored video of himself several years ago in some sort of celebrity joke wrestling match in which he punches a man whose head has been replaced in the photo with a CNN logo.

The airwaves are filled with impotent outrage over this uncivil behavior, as they have been so many times during the past year. Yesterday a smattering of demonstrations around the country called for impeachment. With both houses of Congress controlled by Republicans who are mostly mute after each new outrage, impeachment is not likely, and were he to survive impeachment, as Bill Clinton did, I think he'd feel emboldened to act even more egregiously. Freshman Congressman Jamie Raskin, the former Constitutional Law professor for whom I led a nature walk on Inauguration Day, has taken another direction, introducing a bill in the House calling for an oversight commission of physicians, psychiatrists, and former high-office holders to remove the president if he's deemed mentally or physically unfit to lead, based on the Twenty-Fifth Amendment.

I think it's dawning on many people that there's method to the madness of the current White House occupant. While he distracts the press and public with a steady stream of bullying tweets and inflammatory rallies, he is quietly dismantling and undoing the accomplishments of Obama and previous administrations at the agency level. Scott Pruitt at the EPA is rolling back every environmental protection he can get his hands on. There is already one extremely conservative judge installed on the Supreme Court. If he gets another shot at the high court, a likely prospect, heaven help us.

When I'm in my purposeful naturalist mode, I can stay focused on the good. When I'm with family and friends or out in nature, hope rules in my heart. But, when I expose myself to the news of the day, the incivility of our president, and the heartlessness and cowardliness of the Republican majority on the Hill, eat away at me. I feel compelled to take action but can't find purchase. I know I am not alone in this feeling of enraged helplessness.

"Whither the Republic?" The question I saw scrawled in the frozen snow near the Roosevelt statue on a winter evening isn't a new one. Nor is hope new in the face of it. Roosevelt himself, child of a northern father and southern mother, knew first-hand the shattering divisiveness of the Civil War. Theodore Roosevelt Sr. chose not to fight, perhaps in part so that he would not be pitted against the brothers of his wife, Martha ("Mittie") Bulloch, who were Confederate naval officers. Roosevelt's father cared deeply about the Union cause and made a significant contribution to its success. He initiated a far-reaching program and worked tirelessly to help Union soldiers send money from their paychecks to their families. However, his son, a young boy during the Civil War, struggled all his life with his father's decision not to fight. He charged fearlessly up San Juan Hill with the "Rough Riders," determined to prove himself a warrior, gaining national acclaim that propelled his political career. However, on another level, his was a family united in bridging the country's deep divide. Roosevelt revered his father above all others, describing him, in his 1913 autobiography, as "the best man I ever knew," who "combined strength and courage with gentleness, tenderness, and great unselfishness,"[47] and he also had tremendous respect for his uncles, who inspired his lifelong passion for naval history and power. He described his mother as a "sweet, gracious, beautiful Southern woman, a delightful companion and beloved by everybody. She was entirely 'unreconstructed' to the day of her death."[48]

July 6th: The Kingfisher and Grandmother Sycamore

Today we are getting a good soaking rain. The green of young summer was beginning to lose its luster, but all is lustrous once more. I have been peeking through the curtain in Sophie's room to get glimpses of the dove parent and nestling, who has grown from a gray fluff ball to a sleek young version of her doe-eyed parents in a matter of days.

Watching the doves has given me an appreciation for the dove as a symbol of peace. For days the male and female dove patiently took turns incubating the single egg in their haphazard-looking nest on the window ledge. Then *voilà*! Out hatched a fluffy babe. Each parent in turn and the young dove have been sitting patiently side by side in the crowded nest this week, patiently watching the world, the nestling growing, the dark-eyed parent inscrutably serene. While the nesting jays exuded visibly watchful vigilance, the dove's temperament seems gentler. The next thing I know, one of the doves will fly past the house carrying an olive branch.

On Independence Day, Jim and I packed a picnic lunch and headed for Rock Creek Park in his truck. While driving, we listened to a C-Span interview with the historian David McCullough, who wrote a wonderful biography of Theodore Roosevelt and his family titled *Mornings on Horseback*. During the interview, he called our current president the least qualified person ever to run for the office. At age 83 (he'll be 84 tomorrow), and having received two Pulitzer prizes, the National Book Award, and the Presidential Medal of Freedom, McCullough is a voice to respect.

Wood thrush song filled the trees as we embarked on our 4-mile hike through the summer forest, along the creek that Roosevelt forded many times, and into the upland woods, where he led his ambitious hikes and rock scrambles and rode horseback with family, friends, and colleagues. Our moseying pace would have been far too tame for the intrepid president.

As we neared Boundary Bridge we ran into Marion Werner, great-granddaughter of Charles Carroll Glover, primary founder of Rock Creek Park, and her husband Tony. I told her I'd just been thinking about her great-grandfather, as I often do when I'm feeling grateful for Rock Creek Park. Glover took a group of his influential friends on a Thanksgiving Day horseback ride in the Rock Creek stream valley in 1888, and, steeped in the memory of the beauty of that ride, they all pledged and successfully lobbied Congress to pass the act to create the country's first urban national park in 1890.

Yesterday I paddled toward the island from Thompson Boat Center. Just days away from the completion of my island year of record, who should come flying above my kayak in the Georgetown Channel, almost colliding with my paddle, but a female kingfisher. The kingfisher flew into the branches of an American elm, then flew out in front of my boat again, leading me around the northern tip of the island to Little River. Just as she had done a year ago, she was flying out in front of me, landing on a tree branch, and then taking wing again. After several hundred feet of the flying/paddling dance, I temporarily lost sight of her.

When the kingfisher came into view again, she had landed on a low branch of Grandmother Sycamore's crown. Clearly, I'm not going to feel an imminent sense of resolution on the national or global front. Yet I feel I have witnessed the miraculous in the actions of the kingfisher. The bird, the tree, and the island seem to be speaking with one deep abiding voice: *We are here. Pay attention.*

July 11th: Stubborn Wildness

When I picture Theodore Roosevelt Island, I see a place that is stubborn in its wildness. The island sits entirely within the bounds of the nation's capital, yet is all to itself. In the past it offered refuge for members of the Nacotchtank tribe, for the family of George Mason, and for African American troops and people escaping slavery. Today it is an island no human inhabits, only the statue of Roosevelt with his upstretched arm and halo of granite tablets bearing his words. Theodore Roosevelt was a stubborn defender of wild places, and this island is a fitting memorial to his legacy as a passionate and persistent naturalist and conservationist. On a deeper level, it is a refuge for anyone who seeks direct communion with sheer wild beauty.

It is now a year to the day since I recorded my first encounter with the kingfisher who led me down Little River and back again, inviting me on a year-long exploration of her island home. What have I learned from this tandem journey? As I witness our slow, painful slide into destructive climate change, and try to get a handhold on the gestalt of the times, two things are clear to me.

The first: Vision and inspiring leadership are required to lead us in a remedial direction both for the climate and to promote social justice. Theodore Roosevelt, who ushered in an American century of great optimism, challenged corporate interests when they conflicted with the common good, and sought to offer all Americans a "square deal," spoke these words:

> Of all the questions which can come before this nation, short of the actual preservation of its existence in a great war, there is none which compares in importance with the great central task of leaving this land even a better land for our descendants than it is for us.[49]

If that was true at the dawn of the twentieth century, it is a truth harder to ignore during the morning of the twenty-first.

Roosevelt quoted what he called "a bit of homely philosophy" in his autobiography: "Do what you can, with what you've got, where you are."[50] And he advised: "Be practical as well as generous in your ideals. Keep your eyes on the stars but remember to keep your feet on the ground."[51] I know many people who live their lives cleaved to those practical principles. What's lacking today is pragmatic, creative, and bold leadership at the national level. Unless we elect national leaders who look to our children's future, as Roosevelt did, we may lose our opportunity to protect our land. When Roosevelt declared the Grand Canyon a national monument, there was a huge outcry from Arizonans. During his presidency Joseph Cannon, then Speaker of the House, famously declared he would spend "not one cent for scenery."[52] Yet few would question the wisdom of protecting the Grand Canyon, or any of our other iconic national parks and national monuments, today.

The second truth that is clear to me is that we all benefit when we come closer to nature, for our personal well-being and as inspired and educated stewards. Roosevelt wrote: "it is an incalculable added pleasure to any one's sum of happiness if he or she grows to know, even slightly and imperfectly, how to read and enjoy the wonder-book of nature."[53]

For this past difficult year, Theodore Roosevelt Island has been my "wonder-book." I can't stop fearing for our uncertain future or struggling in my quest to learn what I can do to make things better. Yet this I know: When I'm paddling along the rocky shore, I'm in good company with the chattering kingfisher and the stubborn wildness of her island home.

When Roosevelt reflected on his days as a very young man in the badlands of the Dakota Territory, he declared: "Here the romance of my life began."[54] May the romance of our lives begin here today as we create deeper connections with the natural world. And may that romance deepen, as young Roosevelt's did, into an abiding passion for conservation.

Acknowledgments

My heartfelt thanks to all the nature enthusiasts who walked and kayaked with me on and around Theodore Roosevelt Island during my year of record. "Kingfisher Court" members Betsy Lovejoy, Sharon Forsyth, Tim Reed, and Dave Sperling taught me about the island's birds and helped to lift my spirits after the disheartening November 2016 election and during the ensuing seasons. Wendy Paulson came to town in January of 2017 and gathered up some of her nature-loving conservationist friends and colleagues for a restorative winter walk. Thomas Lovejoy, who was on that walk, generously agreed to write the eloquent and insightful foreword to this book. Botanist Rod Simmons walked with me in the winter rain, identifying grasses and sedges, as well as the island's large Shumard oak. Geologists Joe Marx and Tony Fleming generously shared their extensive and intimate knowledge of Theodore Roosevelt Island and the Potomac Gorge. Kate Maynor taught me nature journaling inspired by her teacher Jack Laws, and Disha Banik delighted me with a spontaneous poetry reading. Thank you to fellow author and nature enthusiast Kristie Miller, and birder and close friend Anne Sturm.

Thank you to Joanna Sturm, Susan Roosevelt Weld, Tweed Roosevelt, and Winthrop Roosevelt for sharing knowledge of your ancestor and love of his memorial island with me. Thank you to the National Park Service, NPS Cultural Resources Program Manager, Brad Krueger, and board members of Friends of Theodore Roosevelt Island—Sam Sharp, Nicole Goldstein, and John Doolittle. Since my year of record (2016–17), I've developed a wonderful working relationship with Clay Jenkinson and Sharon Kilzer of the Theodore Roosevelt Center at Dickinson State University in North Dakota. Each September Clay and I lead trips to Theodore Roosevelt National Park for Smithsonian

Associates, trips that have enhanced my appreciation for Theodore Roosevelt and for the Dakota badlands that helped restore his spirits after his mother and wife died on the same day and inspired his conservation ethic. Other scholars and colleagues who have contributed greatly to my knowledge of TR include authors Darrin Lunde of the Smithsonian's National Museum of Natural History and Char Miller of Pomona College.

I thank everyone who has participated in guided walks and kayaking trips in Washington's wild places with me. You know who you are! Special thanks to Susan Austin Roth, Polly Alexander, Doug Barker, Sadie Dingfelder, Clare Kelley, Dr. Paul Jarris, Ana Ka'ahanui, Stella Tarnay, Brenda Lee Richardson, Julie Kutruff, Sieren Ernst, Gabriel Popkin, and Elana Goldstein, who have shared many inspiring and restorative moments in the field with me. Alan Whittemore, Cris Fleming, Carole Bergmann, and Elizabeth Rives are my forever go-to botany experts. Stephanie Mason has answered hundreds of naturalist questions over the years, most recently about osprey migration. Alonso Abugattas has taught me much about herbal lore.

Amos Clifford and my fellow forest-bathing guides are a perennial source of knowledge and inspiration. The Audubon Naturalist Society, Politics & Prose, Smithsonian Associates, Casey Trees, the Nature Conservancy, the Rock Creek Conservancy, the US Botanic Garden, Friends of Theodore Roosevelt Island, and Capital Nature are among the many wonderful local organizations supporting nature events in which I regularly participate. Special thanks to the Maryland and Virginia Native Plant Societies. I thank my friend and colleague Dr. Robert Zarr, founder of Park Rx America, for encouraging his patients, fellow physicians, and friends to value time spent in nature as a wellspring of physical and mental health. Thanks too to Executive Director John Henderson.

I thank NPR reporter Allison Aubrey, whose 2017 story based on a forest-bathing walk at Theodore Roosevelt Island remains one of the top forest-bathing resources today. I thank Maryland District 8 US Congressman Jamie Raskin and his wife, Sarah Bloom Raskin, for their wise leadership. Special thanks to my dear friend Terrie Daniels for sharing the Wendell Berry poem, "The Peace of Wild Things," with Jamie, Sarah, and many friends in Rock Creek Park on Inauguration Day 2017. Thank you to ethnobotanist and author Susan Leopold for your teaching.

My wonderful agent, Marilyn Allen, and my trailblazing publisher, Tim Ward of Changemakers Books, believed in this book project from the start. Tim simultaneously pushed me beyond my comfort zone and cheered me on to create a much better book. I received brilliant, thoughtful editorial guidance (with some heavy lifting on her part) from Michelle Auerbach, an author, editor, and kindred spirit who lives in Colorado and whom I hope to thank in person one day. Fellow nature author, birder, and dear friend Cecily Nabors gave the manuscript her eagle eye and owl wisdom and to her I'm deeply grateful. I thank Mollie Barker for her excellent copy editing, including Celsius conversion! I also thank the book's talented designer, Stuart Davies, and expert and responsive editorial coordinator, Andrew Wells.

I thank my dearest husband of 45 years, Jim Choukas-Bradley, and our children, Sophia and Jesse Choukas-Bradley, for sharing so many wondrous moments in nature. Sophie deftly edited an early draft of the manuscript and Jesse contributed historical and geographical research. My dad, Michael Choukas Jr., a lifelong birder, and my author/artist/musician/dancer/therapist sister Ellie Choukas Anderson, a forever wild child, have provided constant real-time nature nourishment from New England through the magic of email. Thank you, Tina Thieme Brown, for your wonderful art and another challenging and joyful collaboration!

Endnotes

1. Theodore Roosevelt, *Outdoor Pastimes of an American Hunter* (Mechanicsburg, PA: Stackpole Books, The Classics of American Sport Series, 1990, originally 1905), 339.

2. Theodore Roosevelt, *African Game Trails: An Account of the African Wanderings of an American Hunter-Naturalist* (Middletown, DE: Arcadia Press, 2017, originally 1910), 5.

3. Euell Gibbons, *Stalking the Wild Asparagus* (Chambersburg, PA: Alan C. Hood & Company, 1987, originally 1962), 55.

4. Theodore Roosevelt and Henry D. Minot, *The Summer Birds of the Adirondacks in Franklin County, NY* (privately published and distributed, 1877).

5. Theodore Roosevelt, *An Autobiography* (New York, NY: Charles Scribner's Sons, 1926, originally published, 1913), 318–19.

6. Theodore Roosevelt, *Address at Grand Canyon, Arizona*, May 6, 1903. Theodore Roosevelt Papers. Library of Congress Manuscript Division: https://www.theodorerooseveltcenter.org/Research/Digital-Library/Record?libID=o289796. Theodore Roosevelt Digital Library. Dickinson State University. Theodore Roosevelt, Grand Canyon Speech, 1903.

7. White House Historical Association, *Flight of the Madisons*: www.whitehousehistory.org.

8. Kay Ryan, "Easter Island," *The Best of It: New and Selected Poems* (New York, NY: Grove Press, 2010), 24. Quoting Jon Carroll, *San Francisco Chronicle*.

9. Theodore Roosevelt, *"The New Nationalism" Address at Osawatomie, KS*, August 31, 1910. Theodore Roosevelt Conservation website: www.trcp.org.

10. Thich Nhat Hanh, *Peace Is Every Step: The Path of Mindfulness in Everyday Life* (New York, NY: Bantam Books, 1991, 1992

paperback edition), 10.

11. Terry Tempest Williams, *An Unspoken Hunger: Stories from the Field* (New York, NY: Vintage Books, 1994, 1995), 134.

12. John Muir Laws, author of *The Laws Guide to Nature Drawing and Journaling* in collaboration with Emilie Lygren (Berkeley, CA: Heyday, 2016). Quote is from a journaling workshop based on the book.

13. Theodore Roosevelt, *"The New Nationalism" Address at Osawatomie, KS*, August 31, 1910. Theodore Roosevelt Conservation Partnership website: www.trcp.org.

14. Frederick Gutheim, *The Potomac*, Maryland Paperback Bookshelf Series (Baltimore, MD: Johns Hopkins University Press, 1986, originally 1949), 28.

15. John Bedell, Stuart Fiedel, and Charles LeeDecker, *Bold, Rocky, and Picturesque: The Archeology and History of Rock Creek Park* (USA: Eastern National, 2013), 7.

16. *NIH Record*, January 26, 2007, Volume LIX, No. 2; https://nihrecord.nih.gov/sites/recordNIH/files/pdf/2007/NIH-Record-2007-01-26.pdf.

17. Darrin Lunde, *The Naturalist: Theodore Roosevelt, a Lifetime of Exploration, and the Triumph of American Natural History* (New York, NY: Crown Publishers, 2016), 68. Quoting from the Adirondacks notebooks of Theodore Roosevelt, August 6, 1875.

18. Theodore Roosevelt, "Character and Success," *Outlook* Magazine, March 31, 1900. Theodore Roosevelt Digital Library, Dickinson State University. Quote engraved on the "Youth" tablet, Theodore Roosevelt Island.

19. Darrin Lunde, *The Naturalist*, 68.

20. Anthony Fleming, Potomac Gorge communication shared via email, March 9, 2013.

21. Ibid.

22. Ibid.

23. Darrin Lunde, *The Naturalist*, 68.

24. Leada Gore, *Why Do We Eat Black-Eyed Peas, Hog Jowls and Greens on New Year's Day?* January 1, 2007. AL.com, an Alabama website.

25. Theodore Roosevelt, article entitled "Character and Success," *Outlook* Magazine, March 31, 1900. Theodore Roosevelt Digital Library, Dickinson State University. Quote engraved on the "Youth" tablet, Theodore Roosevelt Island.

26. Henry David Thoreau, *The Journal of Henry David Thoreau, Volume 8, November 1855 — August 1856* (Middletown, DE: Sportsman's Vintage Press, 2016, originally published in 1906), 181.

27. Rachel Carson, *Design for Nature Writing Address Accepting John Burroughs Medal,* New York, April, 1952. Included in *Lost Woods: The Discovered Writing of Rachel Carson,* edited and with an Introduction by Linda Lear (Boston, MA: Beacon Press, 1998), 94.

28. Theodore Roosevelt, *Ranch Life and the Hunting Trail* (Mineola, NY: Dover Publications, 2009, originally published by The Century Company, NY, 1888), 39–40.

29. Jean Jules Jusserand, *What Me Befell* (Boston and New York: Houghton Mifflin Company, 1933), 333–4.

30. William Roscoe Thayer, *Theodore Roosevelt: An Intimate Biography* (Fairfield, IA: 1st World Library, 2007, originally published in 1919), 210–11.

31. Gifford Pinchot to Theodore Roosevelt, undated, Digital Library of the Theodore Roosevelt Center at Dickinson State University: http://www.theodorerooseveltcenter.org/Research/Digital-Library/Record?libID=o188524

32. Theodore Roosevelt, *Citizenship in a Republic, Address at the Sorbonne, Paris, France,* April 23, 1910. Theodore Roosevelt Center Digital Library, Dickinson State University.

33. Melanie Choukas-Bradley, "Worried About the Cherry Blossoms? You May Have 'Phenology Anxiety,'" *The Washington Post* (Washington, DC, March 24, 2017). Online

March 24, published in Outlook section, March 26.

34. George Washington, *The Diaries of George Washington*, edited by Donald Jackson and Dorothy Twohig (Charlottesville, VA: University of Virginia Press, 1976–9), 4:299 (entry for March 26, 1786).

35. Theodore Roosevelt, *An Autobiography*, 319.

36. Robert Frost, "Nothing Gold Can Stay," poem first published in *The Yale Review*, later in *New Hampshire* (New York, NY: Vintage Classics, 2019, first published by Henry Holt in 1923), 34.

37. Susan Leopold, PhD, and Nicky Staunton (illustrator), *Isabella's Peppermint Flowers* (published in Virginia by the author and quoted with permission), 5.

38. Theodore Roosevelt, *An Autobiography*, 327.

39. Ibid.

40. Darrin Lunde, *The Naturalist*, 5.

41. Ibid., 170–1.

42. Theodore Roosevelt, *African Game Trails*, 5.

43. John Muir, *My First Summer in the Sierra* (St. Louis, MO: J Missouri, 2018, originally published 1911. Passage written on July 31, 1869), 106.

44. John Muir, "Mormon Lilies," *San Francisco Daily Evening Bulletin*, July 19, 1877, reprinted in *Steep Trails* (Boston and New York: Houghton Mifflin Company, 1918), chapter 9.

45. John Muir, *John of the Mountains: The Unpublished Journals of John Muir*, edited by Linnie Marsh Wolfe (Madison, WI: University of Wisconsin Press, 1938, republished 1979), 439.

46. Margaret Bayard Smith, *The First Forty Years of Washington Society* [portrayed by the family letters of Mrs. Samuel Harrison Smith (Margaret Bayard), from the collection of her grandson, J. Henley Smith; edited by Gaillard Hunt] (New York, NY: C. Scribner's Sons, 1906), 11–12.

47. Theodore Roosevelt, *An Autobiography*, 7.

48. Ibid., 11.

49. National Park Service: Theodore Roosevelt National Park website: www.nps.gov/thro/learn/historyculture/theodore-roosevelt-quotes.htm.

50. Theodore Roosevelt, *An Autobiography*, 337.

51. Theodore Roosevelt, *Address at the Groton School*. Theodore Roosevelt Collection. MS Am 1454.50 (138). Harvard College Library.

52. Blair Bolles, *Tyrant from Illinois: Uncle Joe Cannon's Experiment with Personal Power* (New York, NY: W. W. Norton & Company, 1951), 120.

53. Theodore Roosevelt, *Outdoor Pastimes of an American Hunter*, 339.

54. Clay Jenkinson, *Theodore Roosevelt in the Dakota Badlands: An Historical Guide* (Dickinson, ND: Dickinson State University, 2006, 2008), 110. Theodore Roosevelt Address, Medora, ND, 1900.

About the Author

Melanie Choukas-Bradley is the award-winning author of several nature books, including *A Year in Rock Creek Park, City of Trees, The Joy of Forest Bathing,* and *Resilience: Connecting With Nature in Times of Crisis.* Melanie brought her love of trees and nature to Washington, DC, following a childhood spent wandering the woods and fields of southern Vermont. She leads nature hikes, tree tours, forest-bathing walks, and kayak trips for many non-profit organizations in the Washington area and in the American West and New England.

Books by Melanie Choukas-Bradley

Resilience: Connecting with Nature in Times of Crisis (2020)

The Joy of Forest Bathing: Reconnect with Wild Places and Rejuvenate Your Life (2018). Illustrated by Lieke van der Vorst.

A Year in Rock Creek Park: The Wild, Wooded Heart of Washington, DC (2014). Photography by Susan Austin Roth.

City of Trees: The Complete Field Guide to the Trees of Washington, DC (2008; 1987; originally published as *City of Trees: The Complete Botanical and Historical Guide to the Trees of Washington, DC*, 1981). Illustrated and co-authored by Polly Alexander.

An Illustrated Guide to Eastern Woodland Wildflowers and Trees: 350 Plants Observed at Sugarloaf Mountain, Maryland (2007; 2004). Illustrated and co-authored by Tina Thieme Brown.

Sugarloaf: The Mountain's History, Geology and Natural Lore (2003). Illustrated and co-authored by Tina Thieme Brown.

CHANGEMAKERS
BOOKS

TRANSFORMATION

Transform your life, transform your world - Changemakers
Books publishes for individuals committed to transforming their
lives and transforming the world. Our readers seek to become
positive, powerful agents of change. Changemakers Books
inform, inspire, and provide practical wisdom and skills to
empower us to write the next chapter of humanity's future.
If you have enjoyed this book, why not tell other readers by
posting a review on your preferred book site.

Recent bestsellers from Changemakers Books are:

Integration
The Power of Being Co-Active in Work and Life
Ann Betz, Karen Kimsey-House
Integration examines how we came to be polarized in our dealing
with self and other, and what we can do to move from an either/
or state to a more effective and fulfilling way of being.
Paperback: 978-1-78279-865-1 ebook: 978-1-78279-866-8

Bleating Hearts
The Hidden World of Animal Suffering
Mark Hawthorne
An investigation of how animals are exploited for
entertainment, apparel, research, military weapons, sport, art,
religion, food, and more.
Paperback: 978-1-78099-851-0 ebook: 978-1-78099-850-3

Lead Yourself First!
Indispensable Lessons in Business and in Life
Michelle Ray
Are you ready to become the leader of your own life? Apply
simple, powerful strategies to take charge of yourself, your
career, your destiny.
Paperback: 978-1-78279-703-6 ebook: 978-1-78279-702-9

Burnout to Brilliance
Strategies for Sustainable Success
Jayne Morris
Routinely running on reserves? This book helps you transform
your life from burnout to brilliance with strategies for sustainable
success.
Paperback: 978-1-78279-439-4 ebook: 978-1-78279-438-7

Goddess Calling
Inspirational Messages & Meditations of Sacred Feminine
Liberation Thealogy
Rev. Dr. Karen Tate
A book of messages and meditations using Goddess archetypes
and mythologies, aimed at educating and inspiring those with
the desire to incorporate a feminine face of God into their
spirituality.
Paperback: 978-1-78279-442-4 ebook: 978-1-78279-441-7

The Master Communicator's Handbook
Teresa Erickson, Tim Ward
Discover how to have the most communicative impact in this
guide by professional communicators with over 30 years of
experience advising leaders of global organizations.
Paperback: 978-1-78535-153-2 ebook: 978-1-78535-154-9

Meditation in the Wild
Buddhism's Origin in the Heart of Nature
Charles S. Fisher Ph.D.
A history of Raw Nature as the Buddha's first teacher, inspiring
some followers to retreat there in search of truth.
Paperback: 978-1-78099-692-9 ebook: 978-1-78099-691-2

Ripening Time
Inside Stories for Aging with Grace
Sherry Ruth Anderson
Ripening Time gives us an indispensable guidebook for growing
into the deep places of wisdom as we age.
Paperback: 978-1-78099-963-0 ebook: 978-1-78099-962-3

Striking at the Roots
A Practical Guide to Animal Activism
Mark Hawthorne
A manual for successful animal activism from an author with
first-hand experience speaking out on behalf of animals.
Paperback: 978-1-84694-091-0 ebook: 978-1-84694-653-0

Readers of ebooks can buy or view any of these bestsellers by
clicking on the live link in the title. Most titles are published
in paperback and as an ebook. Paperbacks are available in
traditional bookshops. Both print and ebook formats are available
online.

Find more titles and sign up to our readers' newsletter at
http://www.johnhuntpublishing.com/transformation
Follow us on Facebook at
https://www.facebook.com/Changemakersbooks